Dog Behavior
The Counselor's Handbook

William E. Campbell

Cover Design

Marin Graphics

Jacksonville, Oregon

Order Information
Dogwise
Item # DTB646
(800) 776-2665
P.O. Box 2778
Wenatchee, WA 98807-2778
email: mail@dogwise.com
Website: www.dogwise.com

BehavioRx Systems
P.O. Box 1658
Grants Pass, OR 97528
email: billcamp@cdsnet.net
www.webtrail.com/petbehavior

Library of Congress Catalog Card Number: 99-96430
ISBN 0-9668705-1-4

Printed in the United States of America

CONTENTS

INTRODUCTION

This handbook is a companion text for *Behavior Problems in Dogs, 3rd ed,* designed for animal health professionals who would like to broaden their counseling services to include behavior problems or, if already in practice, investigate my approach. A work like this usually benefits from details of the author's background, giving the reader an idea of how the concepts and advice evolved to their present state. So, before going into the first chapter, I hope you'll take a few moments to find out where this author is "coming from."

I entered this field in 1967 as a naive, nearly-pure Pavlovian, tempered by behavioristic overtones from Thorndike, Lashley, Watson, Skinner and several European Pavlovian investigators such as Konorski and Krushinskii. As far as dogs were concerned, except for my own (which were special, of course) I had a typical behaviorist's outlook; that is, if I could simply educate owners in stimulus/response principles, then teach them to shake and toss a dandy little 'psycho-sonic conditioning device' (now known as the 'Dog-Master'), a dog's behavior could simply be 're-shaped' to fit the owner's notion of what a perfect pet should be. However, the first couple of real-life family-dog cases I treated laid pure behaviorism to rest, shattering all my tidy, 'scientific' pre-conceptions . Here are some of those realities:

- Family households are lousy scientific conditioning chambers.

- Dog owners make miserable behavioral technicians.

- Unshackled household dogs do not behave or respond to the environment like stantion-bound lab-animals or captive sea mammals.

- Problems like destructive chewing when left alone can't simply be "trained-out" of an animal.

- Vicious dogs cannot be trained to "want" to comply with their owners' desire that they stop biting them or trying to convert guests into tidbits.

Most important (and scary) of all was this; most clients looking for help arrived for consultations fully convinced that, indeed, we could accomplish all of those appealing pre-conceptions... and even more!

In spite of this, here is what was, and still is, the truth:

- Successful behavior counseling hinges on the consultant's ability to motivate clients to *recognize the cause* of their pet's behavior problem, then to *do something about it with insight.* I had to face facts: Success was not in my control, it was in the clients' hands. If they weren't properly motivated, my chances for a new career in pet behavior counseling were about as promising as Custer's venture into American Indian diplomacy.

We all perceive solutions to problems in the framework of ideas formed from our experience and training. I was fortunate to have an extensive background in human sociology, psychology, employee training and motivation. It melded well with the human relations aspects of this field. So, driven by the foregoing realities, my focus shifted away from training the clients' dogs toward educating and motivating the owners; helping them recognize their vital role in problems as well as their own unique power to achieve solutions. When I reached this objective, both major and minor problems in my practice began clearing up dramatically.

Progress was not made without help. Four years of valuable guidance from the founder of the Canine Behavior Institute, Dare Miller, PhD, provided valuable insight about the uniqueness of human/canine co-existence. His emphasis on the dog/owner relationship and his etiologic (I call it 'causative') approach to problems is indelibly etched in my work.

After three-plus years at the Canine Behavior Center in West Los Angeles and several months going to client's homes (after the Center burned from a fire in an adjacent building) I founded the Dog Owners Guidance Service at the Sun Valley Ranch in Los Angeles. At first, our programs went this way: After preliminary orientation meetings with the owners on Monday, we took five dogs a week into our home or comfortable 'canine-cabanas.' Both Peggy and I taught all the dogs, off-leash, a simple ritual, two-minute-long exercise; to Come, Sit, Stay, Heel, Lie Down, and Go to a place and stay until released. Training sessions with each dog were about ten minutes long and two or three were held daily. We also worked on each dog's problem by simulating their home situations as closely as possible during their five days with us.

The clients picked up their dogs on Friday, when they were counseled in the required environmental adjustments, given a customized 'behavioral prescription,' taught to do the snappy, daily ritual exercise with "Tippy," and then sent off to enjoy a blissful new life together.

Our programs were open-ended; that is, we stuck with the clients until they were satisfied, with no added expense. This led to another learning experience as the phones began ringing with reports of backsliding in a little more than forty percent of the cases. As a result, ultimate success required even more consultations on weekends.

A sixty-percent initial success rate was ethically unacceptable to us then, as it is now. So, the 'instant good-dog boarding program' was abandoned in favor of six weekly ninety-minute meetings with all family members.

After starting this new system, our success ratio and, hence, practice statistics, rocketed. During the next nine years we experienced only a handful of unsuccessful cases; and most of those were genuinely hyperkinetic dogs before we learned of and used, with veterinary cooperation, successful medications.

During those years, with rare days off, I sat under the walnut tree at the ranch with a delightful array of dogs, people and problems; became contributing canine behavior editor to Modern Veterinary Practice magazine (1972); wrote "Behavior Problems in Dogs," (1975) and began writing and testing the BehavioRx

Client Education brochures for use in veterinary, behavioral, humane, obedience training and kennel businesses. I also lectured extensively at veterinary schools, obedience and humane associations.

Enjoyable as our practice was, circumstances beyond our control took a heavy toll on ourability to continue at the ranch: Seven acres next door was re-zoned to accommodate a nursing home. This produced unforeseen noise [racket], always at the 'wrong' time. Our business hours had to be drastically curtailed. Social tragedy also took its toll: one neighbor, our local gas station operator, his wife and our super market manager were all murdered. The neighborhood, in fact, Southern California, was getting downright ugly.

Meanwhile, demand for the BehavioRx System Client Education Brochures was growing. Both of our children were grown up and had set out to conquer the world. So, faced with a hard decision, we trained a replacement consultant in the area, subdivided the ranch and sold out. The more healthful climes of southwestern Oregon were irresistible. Once settled in Grants Pass, we marketed our BehavioRx Systems brochures and conducted consultation work shops. We still see occasional clients, but spend most of our time on our telephone HelpLine for veterinary clientele and Internet clients. And writing.

Which brings us to the reason for this book: I receive numerous calls from veterinarians, veterinary staff, pet dog trainers and behavior consultants who have used many of the correction programs described in "Behavior Problems in Dogs." Their common concern is that the advice for solving problems is effective, but getting their clients *motivated to follow through* is another matter.

The Handbook's purpose is to expose readers to the spirit, attitude, and much of the nitty-gritty, involved in conducting 'client-centered' counseling services and fulfilling our responsibilities to dog owners and their pets. Our emphasis is on the very essence of successful problem-pet counseling... the unique relationship between counselor, client and pet.

Unfortunately, this relationship has never been studied, first-hand, by objective, qualified specialists from any academic field. For that matter, even psychiatric practice was not seriously studied until recently. Therefore, the pet professional at this time must rely on writings and teachings of people who work with people and problem animals. This requires that we depend on anecdotal evidence about the benefits (or the harm) that pet owners receive from any of the various individuals and groups involved in the field. Because of this, the concept of "who is qualified" to advise troubled pet owners has been left to various factions and has, predictably, resulted in the same problems faced by the mental heath field in the past——rampant public confusion.

So, a question must now be asked about pet behavior counseling: Who is really qualified; first, to study about and then apply their learning to the field of pet behavior counseling? To answer this, let's consider some important current dilemmas.

Many excellent candidates for pet behavior counseling are discouraged by the idea that they must first have a degree from a full-time university to be considered "qualified and ethical." However, in spite of accreditation programs, at this time there are no comprehensive educational *counseling programs* for this field of people/pet relationships. Further, *comprehensive* degree programs will not be available until objective research is conducted to determine the *specific* education and training required to serve the public interest ethically.

These are not my personal findings or opinions about designing scholastic training programs: They are based on serious studies in mental health counseling.

The Benefits of Objective Research

"Toward Effective Counseling and Psychotherapy," by C.B. Truax & R.R. Carkhuff; Aldine Pub. Co. Chicago, rocked the mental health field three decades ago. It documented how well the public interest was being served by qualified mental health professionals. The study concluded, on average,

- most of the mentally disturbed who received treatment were no better off afterward than those who received no treatment at all. Further, a significant number of patients were actually made worse!

In defense of this noble profession, many highly effective practitioners also were found. Intriguingly, these effective practitioners' success was not due to academic qualifications, school training or *even the methods they used.* Instead, the research showed it was because they conveyed to patients three, basic human qualities; *empathy, warmth* and *genuineness.* These qualities are possessed to some degree by almost everyone!

The study then tested the importance of these qualities: Some non-counselors (mainly psychiatric hospital aids) were given about 100 hours of training in counseling techniques and the art of conveying empathy, warmth and genuineness. At the same time, two other groups were given the very same training:

1. Experienced, successful therapists (mainly psychiatrists)

2. Post-graduate psychology trainees

To test the training's effectiveness after the training, all groups were thrown into the breech to counsel (with supervision) groups of severely disturbed mental patients.

When the effectiveness of the three groups was compared, there was no significant statistical difference between them!

- The lay counselors produced patient improvements *slightly below* the proficient, experienced therapists and, surprisingly, *slightly higher* than the post-graduate psychology trainees!

The study begged the question, Why?

One thing was clear: practical experience, i.e., working with patients in the wards, along with 100 hours of study and enlightened training in counseling techniques, produced successful entry-level mental health counselors.

Next question: Can these criteria be applied to pet owner behavior counseling? Tentatively, the answer seems to me to be "yes."

One important principle the mental health study suggests is:

- Experience gained by working with people and their pets, plus study and training in pet behavior and counseling, may provide valid pre-requisites for practicing successfully, with initial guidance, in pet behavior problems.

Which brings us to another important research conclusion about education and training provided from the landmark Truax-Carkhuff study:

- The study concluded, with great emphasis, that the criteria for academic study and training for counseling should be based on objective studies of *effective practitioners*. As mentioned earlier, this begs for attention at this writing.

I don't claim to know precisely what makes an effective pet behavior counselor, nor do I equate mental health counseling with our field; I only point out what objective research might bring to light about *educational* needs in pet behavior counseling. Until a study is conducted among the many working professionals in pet behavior, (including those who do excellent work but don't write about it) effective educational and training requirements for pet behavior counseling will remain guesswork.

I also don't claim that my methods and style of counseling are the only way to serve troubled pet owners successfully and ethically. In fact, I lay no claim to the term "client-centered counseling." It is from the Truax-Carkhuff study.

Finally, this is not a review of all the various counseling methods in use today. It is meant to illuminate only one path... the one I know. It is my hope that these ideas will convey a genuine concern and respect for pet owners, their animals, and you, the reader. I hope this information helps you to recognize a particular 'attitude' which can guide the way to a rewarding career with people and their pets. That is my hope: But then, in the words of an ancient sage; "An attitude, like a virtue or a vice, cannot be taught... it must be caught."

William E. Campbell
Grants Pass, Oregon

1

DOG BEHAVIOR COUNSELING
THE CLIENT'S PERSPECTIVE

All clients with pet behavior problems have certain preconceived notions about what they are going to encounter when seeking professional help. These are *expectations* and, although they may be based on past experience with other counselors, they more likely derive from what people have read, seen on TV, heard from friends or on the radio. It is important to be totally familiar with client expectations so we can deal with those that are inaccurate. Here is a list of the most widely held expectations we encounter.

- That pet psychology either has all the answers, or is so much 'hokum,' or somewhere in between.

- That the counselor is a dog-trainer, animal psychologist, pet-shrink, animal behaviorist, or a little of each. (This is probably the fuzziest of all client expectations.)

- That a counselor can tell them *why* their pet is misbehaving.

- That something is wrong with the pet.

- That the counselor will straighten out the pet and the problem for them.

- That the counselor will *tell them* how to solve the problem.

1

- That the remedial program will center on the pet's behavior.

- That 'training' will play a major role in solving the problem.

- That your fee will probably be too high.

- That success should be 'guaranteed.'

Later in Chapter 3 you will see examples of how to handle each of these specifically, but first it will be important to consider a broader view of them.

Client expectations are a bit like prejudices. That is, they are usually based on very little factual information, even less experience, and rarely resemble reality. However, they are real to the client, so they must be seriously considered.

The principles of client-centered counseling guide us to use expectations as valuable stepping stones toward building a meaningful relationship with the client; one in which the counselor is seen as:

- Considerate of the client's opinions

- Thoughtful about their problems

- Sincerely motivated to help them toward humane solutions

Unless we can adopt this attitude and deal effectively with client expectations, we run the risk that they will become *negative distractions* later. So, as off-base as the client's ideas may be, enlightened counseling uses them constructively to establish positive client/counselor relationships.

Client Attitudes:

"Attitude: A mental position or feeling about an object, person, animal, situation, etc..." Attitudes are formed by the combined effects of many experiences. Most of us do not even remember many of these experiences, while others may stand out vividly. Here's a personal example:

I regard eating as a "necessary evil." I bolt my food as if I am late for an airplane. I dimly remember, during the depression of the 1930s, the only thing shorter than food on the table was my Dad's temper. After looking all day for non-existent work and coming home to short rations and an incessantly talkative youngest son, (me), my dinners were often cut short by a stern scolding and "confinement to quarters" for the rest of the evening.

Even though the initial memories are not too clear, their negative effect still colors my attitude about mealtimes decades later. In contrast, I have no trouble recalling exactly why a certain type of German Shepherd Dog—one with a sort of *lurky* look—triggers in me an attitude of serious caution: My flesh provided a partial meal for one!

So it is with clients. Their expectations reflect attitudes that are based on experiences and information, both remembered and repressed. Many of these will be extremely important in solving behavior problems. Our challenge is to recognize, then use them to help solve the client's pet-problem. To do this successfully we must often suppress otherwise 'natural' and/or spontaneous responses to our clients' words and actions, and turn their expectations into constructive tools.

For example, when you first meet the client and they hand you the leash, saying... "Let's see if you can handle him!" (and it will happen) you'd be understandably human if you retorted;

"Sorry, he's your problem, not mine."

However, this answer can create stumbling blocks, rather than stepping stones, from the client's expectation that "you" are going to do something to straighten the dog, and training is what's needed.

A more constructive (smiling) response would be;

"Well, that's an idea, but if I work with your dog, it's like letting a seasoned horseman ride the horse that threw you last week. After I get on him and he recognizes I can handle him, then you remount him,

3

> *he's even more impressed with your ineptness——the problem is made worse. However, if we can help you become expert in the saddle, the horse will recognize it and respond to you. What do you think?"*

This answer gets nicely through the expectations and places you effectively in the role of teacher and counselor.

Please note, the counselor doesn't respond by saying,

"Why do you want me to handle your dog?" or, "What makes you think that will help?"

Either of these risks making the client think you are trying to put him or her on the defensive.

In client-centered counseling, our primary purpose is not to probe the depths of the client's psyche to find out how he or she developed certain expectations. That is best left to the mental health professionals, and even they have difficulty agreeing how best to do it. However, it is our responsibility to seek to understand how owner attitudes affect their pet's behavior, because those attitudes guide *how people treat their animals* and, in turn, affect the pet's behavior.

- In client-centered counseling, to ignore this vital aspect of the pet/owner relationship would not only be unprofessional, but unethical.

There will be appropriate times for searching questions like "Why do you say that?" or, "How do you feel about this?," but these usually concern more concrete, emotional elements of the problems than the client's expectations.

Identifying Attitudes

It isn't difficult to recognize other people's attitudes. Their speech and other behaviorisms reveal them. We deal with them constantly, like it or not; from our spouses, children, bosses, co-workers, neighbors, etc., virtually everyone whom we need to "get along with," so to speak. We regularly adjust, or fail to adjust, either inwardly or outwardly, every day.

However, successful counseling requires that we make our adjustments with 'insight.' This can create an atmosphere in which clients perceive problems in a new way——a way that allows them to *change* an attitude when needed and to feel motivated to do things differently to solve problems. This might seem to be very close to the objectives of a psycho-therapist, but we are dealing with people/pet relationships, not self-images, psycho-sexual feelings, etc. Even so, I have seen confusion between the two professions in the past.

> *The film crew for TV show "Bill Burrud's Animal World" spent a full day at our Sun Valley Ranch. They got great action shots——a dog fight, a vicious hyper-kinetic Great Dane frothing at another dog through a fence and several successful correction demonstrations. After the shooting was finished the producers privately interviewed some of my clients. They emerged from the office, drew me aside and said, "You're practicing psychiatry without a license!" The footage never got on the show: It was deemed "too cerebral" for their audience.*

So, client-expectations can help reveal underlying attitudes to the client's benefit— if the counselor uses them with insight. To accomplish this we must approach expectations with a special attitude, as well. Therefore, before we address any specific client expectations, an examination of the counselor's attitudes is in order.

2

THE COUNSELOR'S PERSPECTIVE

Just as clients have expectations about us and our services, so we counselors have ours, and these will vary according to our individual experience and, hence, our attitudes. The difference is that, as 'professionals,' we must not allow our attitudes and expectations to interfere with doing the job of helping clients to solve their problems. This means that we must recognize our attitudes, then reflect on how they either enhance or interfere with counseling functions. Then we can perform our job with consideration for the client's feelings and problems, and with the genuineness mentioned earlier. Only with this insight can we fulfill the requirements of client-centered counseling.

Dogs have evolved with humans over the centuries from co-hunters, tribal sentries, stock shepherds and even food-animals, to the point where they are now treated and perceived as adopted members of human families. The fact that this has happened at all is, in itself, evidence of the dog's unique ability to adapt. In their role as four-legged 'children,' they are endowed by owners with many of the same emotional attachments as natural off-spring; and by the family children as brothers or sisters.

If we disregard these human feelings and try simply to make the dog's behavior the focus of our counseling, we sacrifice two crucial elements for solving behavior problems. First is the owner's *emotional commitment* to solve the problem. Second is any useful discussion about how the owner's *feelings* affect their dog's behavior.

It would be more than pompous to state that I and others who share my perspective have the "right" attitude for pet behavior counseling. It would be absurd to claim that there is some well-defined formula for a successful attitude. However, it will be helpful to point out some of the prevalent attitudes among highly successful client-centered counselors. These attitudes bear on dogs, dog ownership in general, and dog owner-clients.

A Perspective on Dogs

Client-centered counselors view dogs with awe; not fear or dread, but a kind of awe that springs from wonder. The dog's adaptability is seen as an absolute marvel of nature, yet to be fathomed by objective, scientific observations. The canine senses extend beyond the five commonly accepted ones to these counselors. The dog's uncanny abilities to sense time, distance and direction are a reality, and are used extensively in behavior problem programs. Also, these counselors harbor an attitude of near reverence toward the dog's uncanny ability to sense 'emotional aura'. It is seen as interwoven throughout all its other senses. This sense, too, is a vital tool for working out solutions.

These canine powers are not viewed as 'mystical.' They are perceived as real——either because they have been experienced, and/or the counselor has learned about them from sources that created profound intellectual and emotional impacts. And they are not credited to certain breeds over others. These counselors do not harbor breed-gestalts, such as "Irish Setters are hard-headed," or "Dobermans turn on their owners." When it comes to these senses, Chihuahuas and Great Danes stand eye-to-eye.

The third chapter of Pfaffenberger's "New Knowledge of Dog Behavior" is familiar to these counselors. The fact that adult dogs of various breeds and mixes, donated to the Army K-9 Corps by their owners, formed relationships with soldiers and led them through seven weeks of vicious jungle fighting in the Markham and Ramu valleys of New Guinea... without a single man or dog casualty. This incredulous statistic also helped form the successful counselor's attitude toward dogs.

These returning soldiers testified that they depended *totally on* their dog's *judgment* without commands, drank the same water, ate the same food, slept together in the same foxholes, hid from or sought out and killed a common foe; these facts also helped form these attitudes.

Hollow-eyed veterans, saying that their dogs were just as much "persons" to them as the soldiers were to each other, made an enormous impact about the role of a *human's attitudes* and their dog's behavior. Further, every one of these war dogs was rehabilitated to civilian life and lived successfully as a companion pet. Only one mishap occurred——a civilian owner irresponsibly directed his dog to 'guard' when someone approached.

Perceiving that dogs possess these potentials endows these counselors with incredible patience. They operate on the premise that problems spring from faulty elements in the environment that, when put right, will satisfy, rather than frustrate, the dog's fundamental social needs. This goal is not accomplished by applying behavioristic 'protocols' from un-natural experiments or training designs, but by applying real-world experiences, either personal, or from those shared by others.

For example, client-centered counselors understand how futile it is to advise an otherwise subordinate-acting owner to make their dominant-acting dog "Sit/Stay" when its food is put down as a way to establish owner-dominance. If the client has used such an exercise in the past, the counselor with insight guides the client back several steps, to when the dog *starts* to 'pester' for its meal. The client, almost invariably, says they generally respond to the pestering by getting the food ready, then commanding the dog to Sit/Stay before it is placed down.

So the counselor then says;

> *"Well, now, let's examine what happened from the dog's perspective. He pestered and you did what?" The client responds, "I prepared his meal." "OK,"*

9

says the counselor, "who acted as the leader in that scenario?"

The client correctly identifies the dog.

"Excellent. But now, from that point onward, what is dominating the dog's mind?"

"Dinner. . . eating."

"Great. So, what is the dog Sit/Staying for?"

At this point clients have an Aha! and say...

"The food, of course."

Others may not grasp the point immediately and say the dog is sitting "because I told him to."

When this happens, the counselor asks,

"What do you think would happen if you went through all the motions of getting dinner, but put down an empty food dish for several days?"

Even the most rigid personalities usually appreciate that the dog will either stop sitting on command, or will become highly excitable and confused. Then, clients recognize that the dog is Sit/Staying for the food, not their direction. At that point they are ready to ask for the Sit/Stay at pester-time as a response to the dog's demand for subservience (getting the food), then release the pet. This way, obedience is associated with the owner's leadership in the situation rather than with the food itself.

I mention the foregoing only to provide a brief example of how this type of counselor's attitude about dogs manifests itself when introducing clients to their "real" dogs, versus the clients' misconceptions of them.

Attitudes Toward Dog ownership

Having a dog is perceived as the result of cultural influences rather than necessity, at least in most western civilizations. That is, most dogs are obtained only because people *want* them, without a meaningful appreciation for the dog's unique potential to enhance the social fabric of family life. Successful counselors see their role as guides to help individual clients and society as a whole to actually *experience* the long-muted values of dog ownership.

Client-centered counselors do not harp on "responsible pet ownership," especially in a public forum. They understand that many members of today's self-oriented society increasingly reject responsibility, even for the care of their children and parents. Rather, these counselors seek to enlighten people about the very real benefits of dog ownership. In this way the counselor creates living examples of these values that, in turn, spread the 'message' more effectively than proclamations about responsibility.

Attitudes Toward Client Dog Owners

These counselors see dog owners in the framework of each client's total environment, which intimately involves the client's motivation for ownership. In working with owners of problem dogs, they earnestly seek to discover, then to communicate their understanding of these motivations, no matter how naively misguided or mercenary they may be. Only with this attitude can a genuinely constructive relationship be established between counselor and client.

Client-centered counselors do not set themselves up as authority figures with their clients or their problem dogs. They view clients as equal human beings, suffering from the disappointment of having obtained a pet dog whose misbehavior is a reflection on their integrity as pet owners. No matter how deeply this feeling is submerged in intellectual rationale about the dog's breed, temperament, background or other factors, the successful counselor understands the depth and fragility of these client feelings. With this attitude, the counselor can feel *with* his clients, rather than pass judgment or feel sorry *for* them.

Successful counselors avoid projecting the idea that they have all the answers. To the contrary, they hold the attitude that the client "knows, but doesn't *know* that he or she knows," and only needs the counselor's assistance to 'discover' the steps toward a solution. Although clients tend to arrive with the notion that they "know not, and *know* that they know not," (and hence, want to be *told what to do*) the counselor understands that what clients *think* they need to know is not what they *really* need to know. For this reason the counselor's attitude toward teaching varies markedly from traditional teaching attitudes, at least in western cultures. The chapter on counseling sessions puts this kind of attitude into practice.

Teaching an "attitude" is not popular among many behavior consultants today, probably because it has not been written about extensively in pet behavior literature. However, it is extremely effective. Let's examine a couple of examples.

Attitudes Working with Techniques:

The fascinating thing about successful counselors is that their techniques can vary remarkably... yet they can be equally successful. Here are two contrasting examples from partial telephone transcripts. First, a very directive, then a non-directive approach.

"Directivity" with Warmth

The client had a large, 4-year old intact Malamute. He had recently married and the dog was growling at the new wife. The first time it happened when the couple was getting into bed. George became enraged and, literally, picked up the dog and threw it against a wall. No more growling when George was around, but when he was gone the dog would not allow the Mrs. into the bedroom. He also 'skulked' around when George and Annie were home together. Annie weighed just under 100 lbs. Here's an excerpt from the phone interview. It should be mentioned that the counselor had known the client personally for three years. (At this point, George had just finished telling about the history.)

"George, why don't you send Mary to body-building class so she can toss 'Yukon' at the wall? Problem solved, right?"

(George chuckled.) "Wrong smart guy. She's too little and the real problem is that Yukon is dominant with her and submissive with me. What we need is for you to show us how to get her dominant. Then the problem is solved, right?"

"I'd like to be able to say 'Yea' to that, George. We'd save a lot of time. But when I tell you that there's scant hope of getting Mary physically dominant over the dog, where do we go from there?"

"I guess he'll have to go."

"I know you'd have done that before this if you were serious, George. Look, there is a way to solve the problem, but it's going to take some serious consideration by both of you in order to get to the root of it. And that's what my programs are all about."

(Silence, for almost 20 seconds!)

"You're starting to sound dangerously like the therapist who screwed up my first marriage. I'm not ready for any trips into our personal life."

"Tell you what. If I ask anything too personal, just tell me and I'll hang my head in shame. Actually, all we're going to talk about is Yukon's situation. And if that means I have to mention some of the things people do that lead to problems like this, I'll leave it to you and Mary to relate them to your situation. You're mature adults, able to discuss things and make your own adjustments. OK?"

(This answered the client's fears and an appointment was set.)

Analyzing the Interview:

This counselor used an extremely directive, almost non-counseling approach with George, although in the actual meetings with the couple and dog, more non-directive techniques

13

were employed. The case had an excellent outcome. The important thing to note is that even though the counselor abhorred throwing dogs against walls as remedial therapy, he actually treated the incident lightly rather than convey disapproval. Also, when faced with the snide comment about the "therapist," he did not appear defensive. Instead, he was understanding and reassuring, again using humor to make his position clear.

Non-directive:

Next is part of a telephone interview typifying the let-the-client-draw-conclusions approach... highly non-directive.

The married mother of two boys called about a 2-year-old intact male Lab-Shepherd who was urinating a literal water-line inside the house, especially in the parent's bedroom. Her husband had punished the dog severely, to no avail. In fact, the dog had started to growl at him and even tried to bite him the day before this call.

"I don't know what's wrong with Smokey. We all give him plenty of love. The kids will be heartbroken if we have to get rid of him, but this can't keep up. Dr. E. said you were a specialist at this sort of thing. Do you think you can do something with him?" (The client had the 'fixing' the dog 'expectation'.)

"We've worked with lots of problems like Smokey's before and I appreciate your dilemma. Let's get some history. Tell me about the first time you noticed it."

"I think it was around Christmas last year, right after we started closing him in our 10 year-old's room at night."

"Where did he sleep before that?"

"Wherever he wanted, but he usually picked our bedroom. (Pause) But he was getting to be a pest."

"Uh huh. Why do you think he's branding your bedroom?"

"Any time he can sneak in there." (She mis-heard the question, answering "when" rather than "why." However, the counselor made no mention of it at that time.)

"Where does he usually leave his 'Mark of Zoro'?"

"On the bedspread skirt, the side table... he even went on my pajamas when I left them on the floor once."

"He sounds awful upset about something! What do you folks think is going on?"

"We think he's getting even for being kicked out of his sleeping quarters. He thinks he's the boss around here anyway."

"You're darned close to right on that. When did you first think about getting rid of Smokey?"

"Frank said it first, when the growling started."

"I can see why. But it's tough to find a new home for a dog with this kind of problem. Do you have anyone in mind?"

"No. Who'd want him? I guess we'd just have to take him to the animal shelter. I don't know what we'd tell the boys."

"I take it they have close relationship with him."

"Oh, they'd really be torn up. I don't know if they'd ever forgive us."

"You have unusual insight about the implications. Where would you like to go from here?"

"You tell me. But I'll bet it's expensive." (laughs)

> *"Well, I'll explain our program; then you and Frank can decide if it makes sense, and if Smokey and the boys are worth it. OK?"*
>
> *"OK."*

The remainder of this interview covered motivational aspects, the dog's feelings of upset, (including references about his sensitivity to feeling unwanted and that, unless the entire family made a commitment to keep Smokey, a solution was virtually impossible), the husband's understandable reactions, the boy's relationship and the obvious emotional upheaval if the dog were gotten rid of. Finally, the client was allowed to make a decision about a program.

Analyzing the Interview:

Several important points bear on the counselor's attitude. First, he assured the client that the problem had been dealt with before and that he understood her feelings in the matter. When the pest-in-the-bedroom comment occurred, rather than press for details (they usually involve sexual activities) he merely acknowledged it and continued.

Something special happened when she didn't answer the query about why the dog was branding their bedroom. Rather than call attention to it, he merely went on to another needed question, then re-phrased the question later.

The First Meeting

When the husband and boys arrived for the first meeting, they showed an obvious air of; "We're at the dog-shrink because Mom insisted." But when they saw the counselor was a 'regular person,' they said later they really looked forward to all their meetings. Everyone did exceptionally well with Smokey and even referred several friends afterwards.

Controlling versus "Leading" Interviews:

When describing a highly non-directive approach, we don't imply that the counselor does not 'control' the interview. To the contrary, he is in total control. However, his questions do not try to 'lead' the client to favorable (to the counselor) responses; they avoid suggesting answers. He even asks, "Where would you like to go from here?" Which brings the client to a point of agreement to listen to descriptions of the program, as well as the fee. This is also answered non-defensively, placing the decision, (and the responsibility), with the client.

Summary:

The main theme of the attitudes that guide client-centered counseling is; no matter the technique, directive or non-directive, the warmth, empathy and genuineness we stressed earlier are vital factors. We can be letter-perfect in the techniques, but we'll be like Mynah Birds, reciting empty phrases without these three qualities.

There is no script for coming up with that 'just right' supportive comment or the question that will allow a client to answer honestly, make a decision with conviction, or gain an "Aha!" of insight about the causes and corrections of pet behavior problems. The elements required are *knowledge* through *study* and *experience*.

A principle motivated by the Golden Rule leads to single question that can guide the counselor:

"If I were a client, how would I need to be treated."

The *need* rather than the *want* is stressed for good reason. When we look at holding actual counseling sessions, we will see why this is appropriate. In the meantime, the principles of client-centered counseling mentioned thus far, when properly applied, can put the counselor's attitudes in harmony with the client's needs and form the basis for a professional, ethical practice.

Now, let's look at addressing those specific client expectations.

3

ADDRESSING CLIENT
<u>EXPECTATIONS</u>

Let's examine the expectations listed in Chapter One and deal with each specifically. We'll present actual quotations of phrases that are useful, but I do not recommend that you memorize any of these. Instead, if you will concentrate on the ideas behind them, your own style of speaking will create responses that sound natural... hence authoritative and believable.

- Dog or cat 'psychology' is so much hokum; or it has all the answers, or somewhere in between.

No client is going to say this in so many words. You'll sense it from the way they sound when they talk about the problem or the subject itself. You'll answer it effectively by the your attitude, which guides the way you appear and sound to clients.

If a client says, "I've raised dogs before, but this is the first time I ever had to get a shrink for one." Or, "There must be some new way to handle this." (or words to this effect) you have a pretty good indication that they need more information about the field.

The best answer for these expectations emphasizes the real state of the art. That is; this is a relatively new field and, even with all the scientific studies done about dog and cat behavior, we must still design a practical application for these findings to suit each client's problem. There is no "magic pill" for behavior problems. This also ties in with the next notion.

- You are a dog-trainer, an animal psychologist, a pet-shrink, an animal behaviorist, or shades of all these.

This expectation asks "Who am I talking to?" Some clients will simply ask how you got into the field. Some will ask what your "degree" is in or where you went to school. The answer forges an important part of your client/counselor relationship and will help determine the degree of success in all your cases. Formulating an effective response to this question will be one of the most decisive steps you will take in counseling.

Who Are You?

Even if clients don't ask, somewhere along the way in your client-contacts it is wise to answer this question candidly. Otherwise they may make erroneous assumptions about you that could lead to misunderstandings later on. For example, my own writing for veterinary magazines causes many people to assume I am a veterinarian. If the word "Doctor" or some other indication comes up in conversation, I am quick to make clear that "I'm not a Doctor... it's just plain Bill."

In order to answer the "Who Are You?" question it may help if I relate my own situation when I first got into this profession. I had only six weeks to prepare to take over a practice in west Los Angeles which had been staffed previously by several counselors who had not worked out. My background was in designing and conducting management and employee motivation programs for a large US manufacturing firm's international operations from a London, England head office; hardly an impressive history to mull over for a prospective client with a dog problem!

However, my industrial psychology studies and training had provided me with some invaluable tools for dog behavior counseling. One of these was a way of developing a "Professional Inventory" through self-assessment. It refreshed my memory about studies of animal behavior during psychology courses, human and animal motivational studies, plus all sorts of personal experiences relating to dog behavior problems, and my own family relationships involving pets. I hadn't thought of many of these in years. If I describe this, you may find it useful, especially in the early days of practice.

I used the following format to put everything on paper, then studied everything and put it to use.

Writing A Professional Inventory Through Self-Assessment:

It is not possible to design 'form' for this exercise because it might close off too many avenues to strengths. But there are three areas of importance:

1. Dogs:

A. Experience; B. Studies

Write down all your experience and studies: Name the books, describe your duties (what you have done with dogs.) Include family pets, obedience courses, problem behavior actions you've taken, etc... Don't list labels such as "Animal Health Technician." Describe... don't list labels.

2. People:

A. Experience; B. Studies

Same as for "Dogs," but don't overlook your personal experience with people on this one. If you have found that you are a 'good ear' for friends with troubles, list it.

3. People-dog Relationships:

A. Experience, B. Studies

Make the same outline for Cats and other animals in your field of interest.

Use a separate sheet of paper for each of these areas... more if needed. Don't skimp on time. This is *you*, at least in terms of your knowledge and experience in this field. So don't short-change yourself.

When you have completed your inventory, read it over. You'll discover that a review will bring out even more details in most of the areas.

With this inventory of experience and knowledge, the time has come to balance it against the requirements of problem-counseling as you see them now. To do this, use the same format, but list those areas in which you feel you would like more knowledge and experience. This will be your "Self-Improvement Guide." Refer to it as you study and gain experience, transferring further accomplishments over to your "strengths" inventory as they are achieved.

A review every six-months will lead to steady professional and personal improvement.

Now, let's consider what is really on the client's mind:

- What makes *you* competent to help me with my pet's behavior problem?

Very few clients will ever ask the question in such challenging way. Instead, the question will usually be...

- "How did you get into this business?"

This affords a great opportunity to put together an excellent case for the client's consideration, using the following system.

Get another piece of paper and, as you actually recite the answer to that question, make a note about each main point. Review everything several times as you repeat it all aloud.

Next, put the notes aside and go through your explanation and time it. If it takes more than about three minutes, look for ways to crystallize it to get within this time. Try it out on friends until you feel comfortable with it. Ask for criticism and heed it. When you've finished this exercise you'll be ready to address the question effectively for any interested party, including other professionals whom you will be contacting for referrals.

Professional Support:

Finally, list those areas in which you have competent, professional support. For instance, if you have access to a practicing counselor for consultation and/or supervision, a veterinarian for medical consultation, a trainer, an obedience instructor, a groomer, a kennel proprietor, etc. List these by name, address and telephone number. They are all part of the strengths of your practice.

This may seem like an elaborate procedure just to answer one question. However, it will allow you to communicate your answer to clients effectively; i.e., in terms they understand and will appreciate.

Now, to our next client expectation:

- You can tell them why their pets are misbehaving.

During the initial contact with clients this is impossible to answer in detail. However, most behavior problems are the result of some area of frustration in the pet's life. This can be explained with the comment that discovering the answer to this question and designing a "program" to remove the frustration is what your services are all about. Depending on the client's frame of mind, you can also use humor in this "why" category. Here's an example:

A lady phoned about a housetraining problem with her 8 month old, spayed mixed Terrier. Although upset, she did reflect that she had kept her sense of humor, but was running short on patience.

> *"I feed her, take her out, and all she does is pee and then want to play. But as soon as we're back in the house, she sneaks off and 'dumps' somewhere. Now you tell me... Why does she do that?"*
>
> *"Why don't you put her on the phone and I'll ask her."*

This got a laugh, as well as a realization that we'd have to get together and discuss the total situation before the answer could be determined, which we did.

Here is an effective way to put your program into perspective for clients. You can say it in your style, but what follows suits my style.

1. You are going to tell me all about the problem behavior and everything that's going on in daily life with Tippy. When you do this, you will be giving me more than a simple description of the problem——you will be telling me what may be causing the problem as well.

2. I'll then be able to help you recognize why Tippy is behaving as she is.

3. With this information I can help you discover what must be done to correct the behavior. In other words, the solutions will become obvious to you.

Next expectation:

• Something is 'wrong' with Tippy.

Two areas of concern are opened here: first is the veterinary aspect. You can emphasize the need for veterinary examination in order to be sure the pet is in good health, since a pet's behavior is extremely sensitive to health factors. Mention can also be made of possible a food allergy, hyper-activity or even hyper-kinesis.

Once again, you can stress that these considerations are all part of your programs. The word "program" is used to communicate effectively the idea that our services are thorough, as well as to answer a common client expectation not mentioned on our list... that there is some 'quick-fix' solution to problems.

The second area of concern is psychological... that the pet is just plain neurotic. You can mention that although there are cases of genuine neurosis in pet animals, unlike humans, most animals respond much faster to the proper programs. This also opens the discussion to a valuable statement that needs to be made to all clients. You can use your own words, but here is what I usually say in dog cases:

"I'm always amazed at how quickly dogs respond to correction programs that deal with the *causes* for behavior problems. However, our biggest challenge is to get the owners doing the right things. Once that is accomplished, the dogs usually start improving immediately."

This helps instill the idea that the responsibility for a solution is broader than your shoulders—the owner shares it with you. It also supports the pet's genuine capacity to adapt readily to a change in its environment. (More on this aspect later, in answering the "guarantee" notion.)

The You will do it Expectation:

- You, personally, will do something to their dog to straighten it out.

This is well answered by the 'something is wrong with the dog' answers, above. If training is part of your service you may want to explain how you go about it.

Just tell me:

- They are going to be *told* how to solve the problem.

Now and again you will run into a client who says;

"Look... I don't need my dog psychoanalyzed. Here's the problem. Now you just tell me what to do and I'll do it."

As with other expectations, you'll often 'sense' this attitude, rather than hear anyone say it. It usually reveals itself when you find it difficult to get answers to questions about when the problem started, what has been done about it in the past, how the client 'felt' about this or that situation.

One of the most effective answers is to explain that you can only discover what to do if you have a relevant picture of the pet's environment. And the 'keystones' in it are the pet's people. Therefore, to be of any meaningful help, you have to know what's going on around the pet. Unfortunately, the pet cannot tell you! This does not contradict the client, yet supports the idea that they have a role to play.

Fix the Pet:

- Their interaction with you is going to center on the pet's behavior.

This expectation is partly addressed in the preceding one. However, you can mention that pet animals are exquisitely sensitive to the way they 'feel' about their people and other elements of the environment. It can also be stated that pets are closely attuned to the way their human families 'feel' about them. So, to discuss the pet's behavior we have to talk about the emotional aspects of its life as well.

Training does it:

- Training is going to play some role in the problem's solution.

This is a valuable expectation. A complete behavioral program should include teaching clients to teach their dogs at least four simple commands; Come, Sit, Stay and Down. It should also include instruction in the proper handling of the dog on a leash. It is a good idea to mention that the training forms the basis for a three-minute daily "leadership exercise." This provides the client and dog with a ritual that helps to maintain a relationship in which the owner is the leader.

It is a good policy to define the difference between the *deliberate* training of a pet and *correcting* a behavior problem. We can't train a dog not to chew when left alone. To do that we need to find the cause for the frustration that creates the tension-relieving chewing, and then put that situation in order.

The Big Bucks Expectation:

- Your fee will probably be too high compared to the value of solving the problem.

I always compare our fees to the tuition for any specialized, individual, private instruction. Very few clients openly object to fees. Instead, they usually say they'll have to think it over and will call back after discussing it with husband or wife, etc. This is fine, but explain that you'll need a week's notice so you'll be able to schedule meetings that are convenient for the client. For this reason it is also a good policy to require that program fees, like any tuition, are paid in advance. This helps insure that the client follows through to a successful conclusion.

Guaranteed Results:

· You should 'guarantee' results.

Ethically, results cannot be guaranteed, but for very different reasons than most clients assume. I find it most helpful to explain that I cannot guarantee what I cannot control, but I will guarantee to consult earnestly and help plan a program to correct the problem. However, I can't guarantee that any client will carry out the program, only the client can determine that. As in any course of tuition, the teacher may be top-notch, but it's up to the student to earn top grade results.

Summary:

Very rarely will all these client expectations be addressed during a client's initial inquiry about your services. However, if you are totally familiar with all of them, you will be prepared to help your clients form an enlightened perspective about you and your services.

I am sure that you will run into other expectations, since these are only based on my experience. And your situation will probably stimulate ones that are unique to it. However, these cover the most popular notions and should prepare counselors from varied backgrounds with sufficient information to start off effectively on remedial programs.

4

<u>GETTING THE FACTS</u>

At this point we need to mention briefly the two 1999 texts:

- Behavior Problems in Dogs, 3rd ed. - Chapters 2 and 3
- Better Behavior in Dogs, 3rd ed. - Chapter 5

If you've studied these, the following text may seem redundant, but it will be valuable to re-study it. For instance, it will help if you are totally familiar with the Client Record Form in *Behavior Problems in Dogs*.

You'll notice that *Better Behavior in Dogs* includes two types of owners not fully described in *Behavior Problems in Dogs*: 'Jekyll and Hydes,' who display inconsistent emotions to their pets, thereby creating frustration, and Jealousy syndrome types. A familiarity with these and all the other profiles of problem-dog owners will be especially useful hereafter.

Although it is important to understand what type of pet owner you are dealing with in order to analyze particular problems, it should be pointed out that the counseling techniques you might use with each 'type' need not necessarily follow those presented in *Behavior Problems* or in this text. If the principles of client-centered counseling are applied, your own *style* of asking questions, giving supportive feedback or suggesting new or different avenues of thinking or reacting to situations, etc.., will be effective.

Now, "Getting The facts:"

Quantities, Statistical facts:

There are numerous pitfalls built into our spoken language, not only by the words, but by the way we use them. For instance, when you ask someone how old the dog was when they got it, chances are about one-in-four that you will get useful answers. Almost 75% of your clients will say:

"It was just a puppy," which tells you nothing; lots of owners think dogs are pups until they are over six months old. Due to this, when asking questions that require specific information, it is a good idea to frame your questions so that you at least minimize such generalized answers.

Here are a few examples which tie into the Behavior Fact Sheet.

Age: *"When was 'Tippy' born?"*

This is a direct way to determine a pet's age, since it gets a fact from which you can figure its exact age. On the other hand,

"How old is Tippy?" can lead you astray or even require more questions, since the client can answer,

"Oh, I guess he's about two." This can be as much as year off in some cases! And when it comes to determining which developmental stage the dog is in, (or *was* in when problem was first noticed), we need more than a guess. Another good "Age" question is:

"When is Tippy's birthday?" which may have to be followed by... *"And what year?"* to get the age right.

All of the facts about dates and amounts, quantity questions, are most effectively posed so that the client must answer in quantities, dates, etc... for instance, if you know that a kibble-type Chow is fed, *"How much do you feed 'Tippy'?"* is a poor question. Better would be, *"How many cups of 'Chow' do you feed per meal?"* because it causes the client to think in terms of quantity that can be measured and usually avoids answers such as,

"Oh, about half a bowl." This leads to questions about the size of the bowl, etc.., and wastes time, although many times you'll have to settle for the 'bowl-size' when the client can't equate things to cups, spoonfuls, etc.

Questions seeking statistical facts are posed best when they make the client to think in terms of the measures you need for them. This tends to contradict the statement in 'Behavior Problems' which says: *"Never phrase a question that suggests an answer."* Better stated, it would say:

"Never pose a question that suggests a *specific* answer."

This will avoid questions such as,

"Tippy's growling at the visitors must have been pretty embarrassing, right?"

This leads the owner to answer Yes or No. "Yes" is nice and agreeable with your assumption, whereas "No" requires the client to contradict your assumption. Either one is less than desirable.

Which brings up another principle of getting facts :

Avoid questions that call for "Yes" or "No." Although there is nothing wrong with asking if the bitch or dog is neutered, this principle of questioning is most valuable when applied to gaining 'operational' information, which is our next category.

Operational Information:

Operational descriptions are the backbone of effective fact-finding. During initial contacts most clients will be anxious to tell you, in elegant detail, what the pet did. This is vital information. However, it is equally vital to obtain a complete description of what those around the pet did; before, during and after each behavioral episode. This is the area where open-ended, non-leading questions are invaluable.

Example: If the client says the dogs fought today and you want to find out what ended it:

"How did you break it up?" is a lousy question. It assumes that the client broke up the fight, suggests that you think the client should have broken it up and, because of the bias in the question, could close the door to finding out what really happened. It is great question in response to the client's statement that they did break it up, but a poor preliminary question.

A better question is, *"In order to get a picture of what happened, tell me what everyone did before, during and after the fight."*

Even if this elicits more than you may need to know, it will get facts of an operational nature that you can use. Keep in mind, you need a clear picture of the goings-on around the pet(s) as well as what the animals did.

These questioning techniques concern areas of the Behavior Fact Sheet that relate to 'behavior,' not dates, ages, weights, etc... Other facts that are indispensable, though not listed as "emotional factors" on the sheet, concern *feelings*.

Emotional facts:

Clients will convey a great deal about their feelings by the way they sound and the words they use to describe things. In client-centered counseling these facts are of central importance because they are the tools for motivating people toward a solution.

During the initial fact-finding interview, keep in mind that clients do not contact you just because they think you can help them. This is only the intellectual portion of the picture. Most clients actively seek help because they are emotionally upset. This is their motivation.

This is also why many of your initial contacts with clients will contain on all the trappings of a grievance interview about the pet. The client feels any of the full range of emotions and may even swing between two or more of them. At this stage it may seem time-wasting to sit and listen for several minutes to what, on the surface, seems to be irrational, often unrelated elements of a problem. However, the very fact that the client brings them up makes them relevant. So they must be treated as such. This means you may have to ask questions which assure the client that you are interested in them, and which will bring forth other information as well.

For instance, the client may say:

> *"When I got home and saw that pillow all over the house I could have killed the little bastard."*

or;

> *"When I saw that pillow torn to shreds I wanted to sit down and cry."*

These client-statements tell us a great deal about the client's feelings at the time of home-coming, but nothing about what they did. Two elements of counseling, empathy and genuine interest, need to be applied:

- The client needs to know that we understand their feelings, which calls for something to the effect;

  "I can appreciate that." or, "That's understandable."

- We need to know what the client *did about their feelings* of mayhem or despair, which we will probably get without any rationalizing (or downright deception) if element #1 has been communicated effectively. So, an open-ended, non-leading, follow-up question is called for...

  "So, how did you actually handle the situation?" or, "What did you do then?"

If we are lucky enough to get a client-behavior picture, all's well. But more often we'll get an earful about the dog's behavior, which we also need to know and make notes about. It is unwise to call the client's attention to this natural tendency to focus on the pet. Instead, just re-phrase the query about what the client did, after acknowledging the dog-behavior response: Something like...

"I can see how you felt. What were you doing then.?"

This type of fact-finding accomplishes two things:

- It gets operational descriptions of what happened, and

- It helps establish an initial degree of professional, emotional rapport between counselor and client.

Sometimes emotional facts are difficult to gain from clients. Some people make a conscious effort not to reveal their true feelings about other people, pets, situations and (especially) themselves. As mentioned before, it is not our role to "probe the psychic depths" with our clients, but it is important to let them know how meaningful their feelings are about their misbehaving animals. In order to make the point, I find this brief description of *pet emotionality,* and a case story, effective. I'll not present it verbatim, but leave it to you to use your own words, if it strikes you as valuable.

- About 99% of what goes on between us and our pets is emotional. There is very little intellectual exchange between us.

- When you think about it, if they weren't so sensitive to our feelings, we probably wouldn't have them as pets;

- When pets feel emotionally insecure about their relationships with us, they become frustrated and anxious.

- Behavior problems crop up because the pet is trying to relieve the tension produced by some frustration.

Example:

One of the most striking cases involved a lady who called about her Miniature Poodle that had started urinating in the house. He was a year old male. She had gotten him shortly after her older Poodle had died, as a "replacement." She even called the new pup "Alphie II." However, Alphie II was not as warm and affectionate as the late dog. Also, the lady had remarried shortly after getting him and the husband found Alphie II less than an affectionate pet. The lady insisted on coming into a program on the premise that the dog needed re-housetraining and "behavioral modification."

When asked what other courses of action she was considering, she said she and her husband had seriously discussed getting rid of the dog.

The emotional points outlined above were mentioned and she was told that until they made a decision to keep the Poodle, no matter how long it might take to correct the urination problem, she could not be helped. She got very upset, saying that she could not sacrifice her carpets and furniture to a dog's "psychological hang-ups." An understanding for her feelings was expressed, and it was then suggested that she discuss things with her husband, arrive at a commitment to keep Alphie II and then make an appointment for a program. She got furious, saying the counselor was not acting in the best interests of the dog, was not ethical, and had a few more uncomplimentary remarks. She then hung up.

A few days later she called to make an appointment. She said that the urination had stopped! Asked what happened, she said she and her husband had decided to keep Alphie II "no matter what it took." Congratulations were given, but the question was posed: "Why do you need a program now?"

She explained that they wanted to re-name the Poodle and felt they could use some help with a couple of basic commands, plus "things in general." As it turned out, the dog was also a chewer, which had actually led to the getting-rid-of-him idea in the first place. The program went exceptionally well.

The principle of this story has been repeated many times involving almost every type of behavior problem. Simply stated, the principle is:

- When clients change their attitudes toward their dogs from ambivalence between rejection and conditional acceptance to an attitude of total, *unconditional* acceptance of the animal, the dog begins improving almost immediately."

However, experience has shown that unless the owner has that *commitment*, it is extremely difficult to make any progress.

Unfortunately not all clients will reveal their intentions during the initial contact, so it is always good idea to ask them what courses of action they have considered.

The Poodle's case helps make two points. The first is about commitment and pet behavioral reactions; the second is the importance of telling the client something about the counselor's method of working and his or her *ethical standards.*

If you get the idea that your initial client contact involves more than just filling out a form... you're "on track," as they say. This style of initial fact-finding may find you jumping all over the form, making cryptic notes, pausing now and then, maybe even excusing yourself to explain that you are making notes. This is not bad. It tells the client you are interested, that details are important, that you are professional, and that your service will be complete.

OFF Syndrome:

Watch out for what I call the Off syndrome. Off stands for "Officious form-filler." The public is generally fed-up with 'Officials' who solicit information in monotonous, disinterested tones. So guard against sounding like the stereotyped cold-blooded bank loan officer!

Also, avoid sounding 'busy,' or making the client feel rushed. If you really are too busy for the interview, say so and set a time when you can handle things professionally.

Echo:

Another no-no is also a time-waster, especially in the statistical fact-finding phase. It is a habit usually formed by repeating what is being written down in notes. It is usually called the "echo." The professional interviewer avoids it like poison ivy. It goes like this:

"How old is Tippy?"

"He's about 6 years now,"

"About 6 years."

Not only did this counselor ask the question poorly, but he wasted time re-inforcing an inadequate answer!

Another example; this one involving emotional facts:

> *"When I saw the mess in the house I whaled the tar out of him."*

> *"Whaled the tar out of him!"*

This "echo" might not have been so poorly used if it had a question mark intonation. Stated as a question, it would have fit into the category of a "mirror," which lets the client know we heard correctly, but need to know what "whaling the tar out of him" consisted of. Even so, a better response would have been to have acknowledged the client's upset, then to have sought some operational information.

> *"It must have been upsetting to you. Exactly how did you punish him?"*

In any case, it is a good policy to avoid echoing. But the "mirror" statement performs a needed function in counseling. Used properly, it not only lets the client know that what he said has been understood, but leads him to explore further into that area.

Mirror:

> *"I've had Pugs all my life and never had any problems to speak of. But this one is different."*

> *"He just doesn't fit the mold, eh?"*

> *"Right! He won't take a spanking... he even growls when we scold him."*

> *"That could be frustrating."*

> *"Frustrating! It's maddening! Frank said he's going to take a baseball bat to him next time he tries to bite him."*

> *"A baseball bat. How did you react to that?"*

37

This technique uncovered a great deal of contention between the husband, wife and their two children; most of it concerning a feisty little ADR-aggressive Pug. A highly successful program followed.

It is important to note that the "mirror" statement does not just feed back words to the client. It deals with emotions in many instances, such as *"That could be frustrating,"* which dealt with the emotional aspect of the clients words and opened up discussion of the real problem, i.e., the way the wife, husband and kids felt about the Pug. When they understood ADR, PDR, etc., they began working together nicely.

This fact-finding use of the Mirror is not the limit of its usefulness in counseling. If you will use the Study Guide and dig into the Truax-Carkhuff text, you will find it presented in its "therapeutic" context. I do not advise that anyone attempt to become a mental health counselor during pet behavior consult-ations. However, understanding the value of counseling tech-iques will prove a worthy asset in daily practice.

The Dangers of "Halo"

In any interviewing or counseling work we meet people with whom we quickly establish a high degree of rapport; or for whom we hold a great deal of respect, or whose personality and/or professional achievements we regard with high esteem. Because of this, it becomes 'comfortable' to be especially sensitive to their feelings, particularly during the counseling sessions. Where we might press another client for details of a personal nature or an emotional commitment to a course of action, this rapport can cause us to assume that the client 'understands' things without our having to look for feedback or point out misunderstandings.

For our purposes, I refer to this as "Halo." It is almost as if a common 'aura' of agree-ability encircles both the counselor and the client(s). My professional nemeses in this area, for example, are psychiatrists, psychoanalysts, MDs and many of the 'stars' of stage and screen whose work I admire. However, I find halo a problem just as readily with all sorts of clients whose personalities fit nicely with my idea of what a pet owner ought to be!

Often, after a halo-rich consultation, a review of my notes shows that we had a dandy chat, but accomplished very little. I had spoken a lot, they had been super listeners, we nodded a great deal, in other words, we 'halo-ed' beautifully!

I mention this so that you will recognize it. I don't know any technique to prevent it except to stick to your professional guns and follow your principles for conducting an ethical practice. Good luck with Halos!

Summary:

When the principles for getting facts are applied with warmth, empathy and genuineness, you'll not only have the total range of facts you need; you will also have forged the framework for a successful client/counselor relationship and, hence, an effective behavior problem correction program.

Now it will be useful to examine the dynamics of making the appointment.

5

MAKING APPOINTMENTS

Counseling benefits are intangible, unlike houses or automobiles. Therefore, there is really no place for standard salesmanship techniques in making appointments for prospective clients. The initial fact-finding phase is conducted in a way that establishes a positive foundation for a program of counseling. When that has been accomplished, where do we go? Here is the most effective way I have found for making appointments.

Describe the Program - Let the Client Decide

Consider this: The client has inquired about your services. You have told them you need information about the problem and its history before you can advise them whether or not you can be of assistance. At that point you began to establish a counseling relationship with them while gathering the facts. Along the way you were able to deal with their particular expectations. From the client's point of view, a description of your program is about all that's lacking. That, and your fee, of course. So why not go ahead and give clients the facts and let them decide? That's essentially what you'll be doing during the program, so best start the procedure as soon as possible.

Whether it is you or someone you have trained who holds initial fact-finding interviews, whether face-to-face or by telephone, the following method is quite straightforward.

Describe your program in operational terms:

- If they will be coming to your office, describe the place.

- If you go to their home, ask them about it and explain how you will need things organized there. Get down to the nitty-gritty; if you ask that phones be un-plugged during your meetings (a pretty good policy), total family attendance, etc..., let them know. Explain why you need these things as you mention them.

- When describing the program, let the client know what you, they, and the dog will actually be doing. Here' an example from our practice at Sun Valley Ranch.

"We'll have the driveway gates open at your time. Just drive in and around to the back of the house. Bill will shut the gates and meet you under the walnut tree. Keep the dog on leash initially and approach Bill in a friendly manner. This will put "Buffy" at ease in the new situation. You'll will either start off reviewing your problem in the office or with everyone sitting under the tree.

Then he'll explain how your program will be planned. He may want to use the indoor studio or the back half-acre for some simple observations on Buffy's following and other behavioral tendencies. All in all, you'll be spending little over an hour here; most of it talking about the problem, it's causes and the first steps necessary to get the correction program under-way.

He may want to start everyone teaching Buffy to "Come" to you, off-leash, or you may start with "Sit." In any event, you'll be coached in teaching something valuable to put to use at home between meetings. Bill won't teach Buffy anything. We want you to be Buffy's leaders, not him. He might demonstrate a correction technique, then coach you in it, if the opportunity arises.

Experience has shown us that it takes six weekly meetings to gain results that satisfy most clients, which nicely agrees with behavioral conditioning principles for dogs, most other animals, and even people. So we reserve specific times for each appointment. If you have to cancel an appointment, we'd appreciate a couple of day's notice so we can get someone else scheduled. In case of emergencies, of course, we'll be as flexible as possible. Our fee is $___ payable on the first meeting.

Is there anything else you'd like to know?"

(Remain Silent Until The Client Responds!)

Wait for Questions:

This is a critical time. You've spent about 90 seconds explaining things, so they need time to mull over your statements. We've had people remain silent for more than a minute, and then say, "When can we start!" More often, they'll have questions. These may then be answered, after which you can merely fall silent and await the next one.

When all questions have been addressed the client will usually ask for an appointment time, or say they'll have to think it over and call back. Most call-back people have genuine reasons, ranging from discussing the fee with their mates, to just getting off the phone because they don't like something about your program or they don't want to spend the money. Whatever the reason, I have found it a rewarding policy to make the following points before closing the conversation.

- Tell them you usually need more than a week's notice for an appointment time, but that you do have some time on such-and-such, (an earlier day, if one is available). This helps let the client know that your services are in some degree of demand.

- Give them some sort of interim advice... FREE! Make it brief and give them a tip that will be of practical value and easily put to use. For instance, if it's a housetraining

43

problem and they have the dog on demand, or once-a-day feeding, suggest that they change to twice (more with puppies under 6 months of age) a day feedings. Explain why you are making the suggestion, thank them for calling, say you hope to hear again from them and say good bye.

Almost 70% of the clients referred by veterinarians enrolled in behavior programs when these fact-finding and appointment making methods were used. This may not equal high-pressure sales statistics, but the procedures are ethical and they lead to more successful programs for clients who make the decision to enroll.

Finally, for those who make appointments, it is a good idea to send a brief note confirming the date, day and time and any other directions needed. As we'll mention later, it's also the time to either phone or drop a note to the referring veterinarian or other party.

Which brings us to the actual organization of counseling sessions.

6

ORGANIZING THE MEETINGS

Who Should Be There?

Programs are far more effective if all those who live with the dog attend meetings. This requires working weekends and many evenings to accommodate families with school children, but the results are worth it. When everyone concerned in the problem sees, hears and does the same thing with the pet, a general spirit of cooperation about solving the problem is far more likely to be established. Compare this to Mom or Dad attending alone, then going home to try to interpret things for everyone else! In the first place, the parent is hard-put to remember all the details. Secondly, they cannot counsel with your expertise to gain understanding and *commitments* from others. More often than not, they wind up in disputes with family members about new perspectives and some of the techniques involved.

Having everyone attend also has the advantage of seeing how the dogs interact with each individual rather than relying on descriptions. When this is explained, most clients will make special arrangements to have everyone there.

As stated before, clients need an 'operational' description of what they will be doing during the session. This helps to relieve stress for them. Otherwise they are left to imagine what is going to happen. In the end, you will find *your way* to organize comfortable consultations. However, I will describe my own system and leave it to you to use what appeals. Then you can organize and put together your own program description.

THE SETTING

Whether in the client's home or your office I have found certain things necessary for a really satisfactory counseling session.

Seating:

- As many chairs, couches, benches or sofas for all attending, especially if children are involved. These need not be fancy... just adequate. If you can do it, arrange seating in a crescent shape so that nobody is directly facing anyone else. This puts people somewhat side-by-side, more friendly than sitting face-to-face. If you can, leave enough space so the dog can sit or walk between the seating. However, be sure to leave that space between your own chair and the others, especially when an aggressive dog is involved!

Counseling Area Space:

- For the counseling portion of the session you'll only need enough room to accommodate everyone, including the pet. Again, for aggressive dogs I'd recommend an area that accommodates the 'approach distance' for most dogs. My rule of thumb is: 1 and 1/2 times your own height.

Training Area Space:

- For the 'training' exercise section, a minimum area of 20 by 20 feet is needed. This allows room for people to get far enough away from the dog to attract it when they crouch to clap and praise, or walk away, both of which are useful exercises.

EQUIPMENT

I'll list the equipment along with notes about its use. More complete descriptions are in the Behavior Problems in Dogs-3 and Better Behavior in Dogs-3.

Tennis or rubber balls:

- Helpful for 'warming-up' to many aggressive or shy dogs when used by clients for fetching, then handing to counselor for use. Also for noting leg & hip movement in larger breeds who may show rotation, indicating possible hip dysplasia symptoms. When bounced or rolled toward Pekes, Lhasas, and other sometimes myopic breeds, it may show possible perception problems. Sometimes helpful with kennelosis to warm up the dog. Can be useful for bossy dogs who won't give up the ball, when two or more can be used.

Chew toys and squeaky toys:

- Useful for fetch when a ball doesn't work. Otherwise, gives dogs an something to do during counseling session.

Small and medium size stuffed toy dogs and cats:

- These can be helpful for dog-fighting cases. A small one that moves by battery power with remote control is super.

Large black silhouette cut-out of a dog, side view, tail up:

- This can be pinned up on a wall outdoors at least 30 feet away from the dog's entry point to the area and used as a barometer for dog-dog aggression/shyness.

Stainless steel water bowl:

- Empty when clients arrive and used as 'bridge' for the counselor with the thirsty dog.

Collars:

- It's a good idea to have on hand the full range of sizes in flat fabric or leather buckle collars. This allows you to demonstrate the advantages of each as they apply to coat-types and uses. Gentle Leader, Halti, or other lead-restraint halters. Harnesses, if you use them.

Six-foot leashes:

- Two each of heavy and light weights. For training sessions and use with aggressive dogs when the owner shows up with those flimsy supermarket leashes.

Large-brim and/or high-dome hat:

- Helpful with some aggressive or fearful dogs when used properly with the 'Jolly Routine.'

Flashlight:

- For use with light-sensitive dogs and for night sessions.

Cap gun:

- Excellent for testing deaf dogs and noise-shy and sound-phobic cases.

Voice-actuated, battery powered tape recorder:

- This is optional, but I found it helpful in reviewing sessions. Always ask client if they have any objection. Use it for *all interviews you have with the press* . That way, when the story comes out full of distortions, you will be able to set the record straight!

Clothing:

- It depends on your setting and the 'norms' for your own area. However, I do recommend 'Hush-Puppy' type shoes for agility; and loose, long-sleeved shirts of tough material if an aggressive dog is to be seen for the first time.

A Door:

- Any door can be used to ascertain if dog barges out when owner tries to go through. Also for teaching the client the correction procedure.

A Gate:

- Same as for door. A see-through gate is also helpful for aggressive and dog-fighting dogs, animal killers, etc...

Sliding glass door:

- As for gate and door, above.

Other dogs:

- I used our dogs extensively as distractions in most of my programs. Excellent for testing the strength of orientation between client and dog as well as in fighting cases (with fence or door between dogs) with the 'Jolly Routine.'

Thermos with plastic cups:

- Fresh, cool water for everyone is a must, including the dog.

Cellular telephone:

- This is a must for security, especially if you go to clients' homes. Make sure it has a "Panic 911" button with the capacity to report your location!

Telephone answering machine:

- Get one that allows you to call your own number from a remote phone and pick up your messages, especially if you counsel in clients' homes.

Video camcorder:

- This is a luxury, but it gives people insight about the way they 'move' with their dogs during off-leash sessions. Clients usually get a good laugh when they see themselves following the dog!

35mm still camera:

- Another luxury, but I always took 'graduation' photos of my clients and their dogs and sent them a copy.

Clipboard and pen/pencil:

- Excellent for note-taking and clipboard can be useful if dog attacks.

Wristwatch:

- This may seem too obvious to mention, except that I have forgotten mine at times! Use it to time clients during their ritual exercises with the dogs.

Printed materials:

- Business cards, of course. Also, I recommend giving one or more of the BehavioRx System instruction brochures relating to the problem involved. This gives the client a point of reference when questions come up between meetings. Some consultants include a copy of "Better behavior in Dogs-3" 1999, as part of their literature, in with the fee.

Certificate

- I also recommend a 5x7 inch, framed "Graduation Certificate of Behavior Excellence." Most clients give these prominent display in their homes. They can lead to client referrals.

There is other equipment you may find useful, but these have proved adequate in my experience. We use the Bio-Sonic Beanbag in many training and correction procedures. Programs can be conducted satisfactorily without them, but Bio-Sonic speeds up training and corrections markedly.

Now, with the people and equipment organized, it's time to deal with the dynamics and details of the actual counseling session.

7

COUNSELING PROGRAMS

Before going into detail about the general format and the actual content of counseling programs, let's consider an old maxim about teaching; because we are actually teaching, even though we use counseling techniques to accomplish it. The following quote from a Sufi master best describes the type of teaching that will create an change in attitude by students, as well as the motivation to learn new information. At the same time, this saying requires that we put our own reasoning to work, if we are to grasp its subtle messages and gain the maximum benefit from it. As mentioned before, this is not generally accepted in the Western world as a teaching philosophy. However, it describes so elegantly the climate of pet behavior counseling that I have found it to be an invaluable guide.

The Essence of Teaching

"You have to learn how to teach, for man does not want to be taught.

First of all, you will have to teach people how to learn.

And before that you have to teach them that there is still something to be learned.

They imagine that they are ready to learn. But they want to learn what they imagine is to be learned, not what they have first to learn.

When you have learned all this, then you can devise the way to teach.

Knowledge, without the special capacity to teach is not the same as knowledge and capacity."

When we apply the spirit behind these words to counseling troubled pet owners, an 'order' for meetings emerges. My interpretation results in a series of functions arranged so as to meet the maxim's objectives and make up a format. Things rarely take place in strict order during programs, but a total familiarity with the format helps keep things on the right track.

1. Demonstrate that you have new knowledge about dogs and/or their dog and problem that makes sense to them, yet never occurred to them. (Usually applies only to first meeting.)

2. Give them the opportunity to relate other new information to their problem. Then, praise their efforts and deductions by reinforcing their 'discoveries.' Use a brief case example similar to theirs, if it is appropriate.

3. Relate more principles and case examples that will allow them to associate their experiences and problems, opening avenues toward a realization of the causes for their problem.

4. Guide them to 'experience' some of the symptoms of the basic causes for their problem.

5. Outline the principles required for correction which are based upon those causes so far established.

6. Allow them to suggest ways to put these principles into practice in their daily life with the dog. Reinforce appropriate ideas. Guide them positively back on track when their ideas are not correct.

7. Coach them in correction techniques, when possible.

8. Coach the simple training exercise for the week.

I'll leave it to you to relate all of these to the "teaching" maxim. I find it a valuable exercise. Some examples follow. I hope they will provide the same value for you. You will also find variations that better fit your style of counseling. Meanwhile, let's examine an actual case and a session of mine to see how the format was applied.

The Case:

This one involved chewing in the house, general unruliness, sexual mounting, emerging aggression toward outsiders, and growling at the wife when she was scolding and trying to get the dog out of the kitchen.

Mother, father and 16 year old son arrived and drove to the consultation/training area with their 13 month old, in-tact male Labrador Retriever. The dog had barked furiously at me from the back seat, while the son pulled on the leash to keep him away from the half-opened window. I was standing by the front gate to close it behind them. The clients had been instructed to keep "Blackie" on the leash and approach me as if we were old friends meeting again for the first time in years.

I was sitting on the end chair when they 'Jollied' their way toward me, but Blackie strained toward the trunk of the walnut tree, a choice urine branding spot for dogs.

> *"Hi. I'm Bill. Jack! Don't let him pee there right now. OK? Good lad!" The boy looked surprised, but pulled Blackie away and came over to join Sharon and Ralph, who had already sat in the chairs to my right. Jack sat next to his mother. The dog strained to get a sniff of me. Blackie looked much more curious than aggressive, so I said, "Loosen the leash little and let him get my scent. He'll probably relax then."*

Blackie came for the normal smell routine, first my legs, then a wind-scent for my breath. I leaned a little forward (but not toward his head) to help the ritual.

"It's interesting... but dogs and horses are a lot alike when it comes to getting to know someone. They seem to appreciate a sniff of the essence of life, our breath."

"Is that so?" Sharon commented.

Blackie started whining and nudging each of the clients.

I said, "I know he wants to urinate like crazy, but rather than let him do it here, take him back over to those bushes by the fence. Leg-lifting is a canine muscle-flexing, especially if they feel aggressive. So let's have him do it there, rather than here. That way, you're telling him where to go, which helps put you in a leadership role."

"No kidding?" Ralph sounded a little skeptical, but interested. Jack and Blackie headed for the bushes which were some 60 feet away. After about three 'shots' I said:

"He's going to want to have a BM, too, Jack. Let him do that there, too, will you?"

"I doubt it. He went just before we left home." Ralph was now participating, even if being a bit contrary. He showed genuine surprise when Blackie squatted and defecated.

"How did you know he'd have to go?"

"Like people, the nerve center for urination and defecation is shared in dogs. When they get over-stimulated, excited, both the bladder and the bowels get the urge. And Blackie's tail crinks a little when he really has to go."

"I'll be darned." Ralph looked at Sharon with raised eyebrows, I was making some notes as Blackie towed Jack back to our area. Jack sat down while the dog fretted about not being able to sniff out the territory.

"We'll let him loose in a few minutes, after we've reviewed some things here. We can play with a ball and then give him some water." I said.

I then asked each of them about their daily schedule of life with the dog, letting everyone chip in about their activities in the morning, feedings, toilet trips, play, homecomings and goings, sleeping place, etc; getting a general idea of Blackie's life. Sharon spent the most time with him, but exerted the least control.

The play question revealed strenuous roughhousing, mostly by Jack, but some with Ralph at homecomings. Several times they had to punish Blackie in order to calm him down when he'd bite too hard. This type of play started at about 10 weeks of age, shortly after they got him at 8 weeks.

Meantime, Blackie was getting up, alternately nudging each family member, who responded with a few pets, then they told him, "Go sit down, Blackie!"

After the third round of this action, I commented;

"I'll say one thing for Blackie. He's a smart dog."

"Why do you say that?" Ralph looked quizzically at me.

"Jack, if you'll take off his leash and toss this ball for him, we can discuss that. Let's see if he'll fetch for us, or if he'll get us throwing it for him." I flipped the ball to Jack and, sure enough, Blackie fetched it, but wouldn't give it up. He growled when Jack tried to pull it out of his mouth. Jack started to hit him on the snout.

"Don't smack him. Here, take this other ball and toss it." Almost predictably, Blackie dropped the first ball and went after the second.

"Grab that first ball, Jack, and do it again."

After a few repetitions Blackie was dropping the fetched ball and waiting for the next one.

Ralph sounded a little cynical when he said;

"That's kind of a back-door way to get it done. I'll bet he still won't give up the ball he brings, though."

"You're on, Ralph." I said. "Jack, toss me the ball, will you?" When Blackie came back I was bouncing the other ball and he came right over to me. As I cocked my arm to throw said, "Blackie, Give." He dropped the fetched ball and I tossed the other. About four of these routines and I felt ready to put the second ball behind my back rather than bounce it.

When Blackie got back, I held my hand, palm up, under his snout, and said "Blackie, Give." As I said the word 'Give' I snapped my fingers with the other hand. I caught the dropped ball and instantly said, "Good dog," as I tossed it again.

Ralph opined, "I'll be damned. He didn't even growl!"

"No need to. No contest." I replied. "Anyway, he's got to be thirsty now. If you'll all get up, I'll take the water bowl down to the faucet and give him a drink. Water's a great bridge to friendship with a dog. It'll help us get better acquainted if you'll just stand here."

We all stood and I took a relaxed walk over to get the bowl with Blackie tagging along, tail wagging. When I had covered the 40 feet to the faucet, he was jumping at the bowl. I poured it full, put it down beside me and stood still. Blackie slurped his fill, then did what many dogs do; he 'bunted' my leg with his snout (a common canine 'thanks') and we headed back for the group. After we all sat down, Blackie was given a Nylabone and we started the 'causative' and 'planning-the-corrections' portions of the session.

I felt we had started to show that

• "there is still something to be learned"

and had begun to motivate the clients toward...

- "Learning how to learn" and "Wanting to be taught," the first three of the maxim's teaching messages.

Now the job was to get on with presenting the framework of what...

- "they have first to learn, rather than what they imagine is first to be learned."

General Behavioral Principles and Getting Down to Problems:

Laying the background for the problem-causes requires that the counselor relate the principles of canine behavior which apply to each case. Everyone develops their own style from knowledge and experience. So, rather than reproduce the words I used in this case (they'd be quite different for different types of clients, even with the same problems, breed and type of dog). I'll list the 'areas' covered and the clients' reactions to the information.

Throughout the session, this principle was applied:

Principle of Praise:

Praise the client(s) whenever they make the right choice. If not correct, avoid saying "Wrong." Instead, say something like "That's a thought. Any other ways?" Etc...

Elements of Discussion:

1. Leadership capacities of all dogs, wild and domestic. That is, they all are born with the capacity to lead other animals, including the human variety. But they also have the capacity to recognize and follow leaders. Teaching leadership principles and their applications is at the core of our correction programs. The clients nodded, with no comment.

2. Stimulus-response patterns between most problem dogs and their owners... "who's doing what for whom, etc..." The clients related this to the ball-fetch nudge-pet examples already experienced.

3. The frustration suffered by a dog who feels "Leader" in its daily life.

Examples: He can't get his own food, water, chase away all territorial invaders, open doors, or keep the pack members together——all of which are part of his basic 'drives,' at least to some degree. Relate the frustration/tension-anxiety connection.

4. When asked about who goes through out doors first, leash-straining,' etc., these clients quickly related these to the leader-ship concepts.

5. Ask one of the clients (preferably the least talkative) how they might use Blackie's constant nudging for their attention and "turn-around" this stimulus-response pattern to one in which the client can be regarded as 'leader.'

Sharon quickly caught on to this, commenting that if she got Blackie to Sit, maybe he'd quit jumping on her so much. This opened the way for an explanation about making sure that Blackie needed to learn to sit when asked but not to quit sitting until released with an "OK."

Fortunately, Blackie started some nudging, first with Jack, then the others, so we got a chance to put the routine into practice. The clients were tickled with the results, especially when Blackie went back over to his bone and quit pestering without being commanded in any way.

This led to an opportunity to talk about the desirability of having a self-controlled dog, versus one who has constantly to be told to behave. Everyone agreed that self-control was a better way.

6. The nature of the *emotional* relationship between people and their dogs compared to the intellectual relationship: Every-one agreed; it's 99.9% emotional.

The idea of using of a ball and water with visitors for aggressive dogs proved helpful in Blackie's case, since everyone had seen them used earlier in the session.

Sharon thought she could even conduct this exercise whe
was home alone with Blackie. No biting had yet occurred, jusι
defensive barking. Only on two occasions had anyone seen
hackles raised, these were both responses to a teenage boy who
'barked-back' at Blackie. Jack said he could coach his friends in
the ball routine and the 'Jollies.'

7. The functional nature of the dog regarding territorial and
pack protection and the value of a simple daily (preferably AM)
ritual exercise, helping fill the dog's need to function for leadership rather than feel responsible for everything himself.

Everyone saw the value in this, so the exercise for teaching
Come, Sit Stay; and Down, along with loose-leash walking was
outlined for them. Ralph said he'd have to see Blackie walking
on a loose leash before he'd believe it. This brought up the next
area for discussion.

8. The 'language of dogs' in terms of movement (or no
movement), stance, posture, plus their emotional content.
Examples of crouching to communicate "Come," staying
stock-still to teach "Stay," etc...

It was then suggested we try the Come, 'social-barometer'
"back-and-forth" exercise. Everyone seemed enthusiastic and
we'd been sitting almost 45 minutes, so we positioned each
person at the corner of a triangle with about 30 feet between
them. Blackie first followed Sharon, then went over to Jack as he
walked to his position, but didn't follow Ralph.

Each client took turns calling "Blackie, Come," then immediately crouched, left side toward him clapped hands and happily
praised, "Good dog, Good dog," until he came to them. After
brief petting, they stood up and the next person did the same.

When Ralph's turn came, Blackie's approach was cautious,
whereas he raced to Sharon and Jack. We had to coach Ralph on
sounding happy on the command and the praise, but as soon as
he did, Blackie sped up dramatically.

Afterwards I asked about Blackie's caution with Ralph. As
usual, it turned out that Ralph had administered some heavy
punishment on the dog for chewing and charging at visitors. This

brought up the chewing problem, so we went back to sit down and discuss it. Blackie got some more water and lay down for a nap.

8. The emotionality of homecomings and leaving, which dovetails into describing the concept of 'emotional leadership' versus physical or command-control of behavior. This also involves mentioning the 'sensuous' nature of the dog and the way we pet them, along with the fact that the dog who demands and gets non-earned petting will tend to over-miss his people when left alone.

Sharon was especially quick to pick up and relate this, since it was mainly her clothing and her chair which Blackie targeted for destruction. We discussed how to behave when leaving or coming home, what to do when Blackie may chew something, using the Nylabone as a play tool and leaving it, etc. Sharon was taking notes on a pad—a good sign.

9. Re-cap the session briefly and give the clients supportive literature. Explain the probability for progress, then back-sliding. Congratulate them for excellent effort, give Blackie a pat, if appropriate, and see the clients to their car.

10. Sit down immediately and make post-meeting notes about attitudes and behavior of each client and dog's behavior. Don't trust memory. Make notes in code when sensitive matters are involved, i.e., about personality types of clients, etc...

This session did not allow time for the leader-follower exercise and its application to walking on leash. However, subsequent meetings worked on these and the six week program was a notable success.

First Meeting Summary and Review:

All the objectives hoped for were not reached in this session. But an atmosphere was established for constructive learning by each of the clients. Try referring back and forth between the interview format and the interview yourself; make notes where you think improvements might have been made.

One thing I know was a little rough; I failed to work in the causes for chewing at the most appropriate time. I also failed to answer Ralph when he asked why I said Blackie was a smart dog. I hoped that the dog's response to the ball-fetch routine would answer it with actions. Perhaps it did, because Ralph didn't pursue it further. I'm glad he didn't. It was probably a bit too early in our relationship to be chiding the clients, even if in good humor.

Actually, I said Blackie was smart because they had given him three commands at once, backwards! "Go Sit Down, Blackie."... and he got two out of the three, each time. We did talk about command techniques in the second meeting and I mentioned Blackie's "smarts" then.

I guess "perfect" counseling sessions come along about as often as immaculate conceptions. However, even with its faults, this one gives an example of the general "track" I find successful.

These principles are followed during the six-meeting programs with nearly all my clients. However, more time is spent consulting as the programs proceed, since the actual work with the dog gets quicker and easier as the clients improve their leadership skills.

Also, there is usually some backsliding in the problem areas that requires more counseling and less dog-work. The sessions center around the backsliding, client actions and reactions, in order to get at causes and proper corrective steps. This session, and others you have read and will review from the other texts, should allow you to get a firm grasp on applying the principles of client-centered counseling.

Dynamics of the Six-Session Program:

First, a truism: *"No two programs will be the same."*

The reason for this, of course, is that no two situations will be the same. The people, animals and environments will vary widely enough that, even though common problems are being addressed, the program contents will never lend themselves to rigid schedules or identical systems.

For instance, even with regard to teaching dogs the basic, daily ritual exercise of Come, Sit, Stay, Heel, Down and Go (to a place and stay until released), the family with only two members will usually progress more predictably and generally faster than a family with two adults and four teenagers. However, I have also seen things go rapidly with extremely close-knit, highly motivated large families.

Other dynamics, or 'forces,' working against rigid schedules are those *expectancies* we have to deal with. Some clients will not need, or want, or be able to teach all the elements of the daily exercise. So, setting goals in 'stone,' so to speak, might be anti-motivational for them. For these reasons I never suggest printing a schedule of events for six-session programs.

However, somebody had better have a handle on what sort of progress is to be expected, and what goals are achievable during the program. And it had better be the counselor. If not, both the clients and the counselor may find their motivation flagging due to a lack of insight about progress.

Setting Objectives:

I like to define Objectives as "Attainable goals." Nothing is more frustrating than trying to achieve things which lie beyond the limits of reality. Also, few things are more frustrating than having other people arbitrarily set goals for us.

Our sample meeting with Ralph, Sharon and Jack did not allow enough time for them to set their goals for Blackie's behavior. We were too involved in evaluating the situation and getting everyone interacting with Blackie and discussing the problems. However, after our review of the first week's events on the second session, we did get to it.

The Time for Objective-Setting:

The most workable principle states:

- When the counselor has evaluated the clients, the pet, the relationships and other environmental influences, clients should be guided to decide on "achievable goals" for the pet's behavior and their relationship with him. This point is usually reached toward the close of the first session and should not be delayed beyond the first few minutes of the second meeting.

How to Set Objectives:

Ask the client to set them, without influencing them. The most effective way I have found is to say something to this effect:

"Well, we've got a good idea of Blackie's situation now. But let's look ahead. I'd like each of you to give me picture of how you'd like him to behave. Sharon, since you spend the most time with him, let's start with you."

As the client speaks, make notes, acknowledging comments and clarifying points as needed. It is interesting that most clients will have to be guided to give operational descriptions of how they want the dog, literally, to behave.

For instance, Sharon started out with, "Oh, I don't know. I just wish he'd quit jumping and chewing and be a nice dog."

To which I said, "That's understandable. But what would you like to see him actually doing? For instance, rather than jump, how would you want him to behave?"

"You mean, do I want him to sit instead of jump?" (I nodded) "No. He doesn't have to sit. If he just came over, got a pat on the head and went away, I'd be happy."

"That sounds both reasonable and possible to me..."

63

> *Sharon interrupted saying, "I also don't want any more growling when he gets scolded."*
>
> *"Good! Let's look at what he does that warrants scolding. If we can eliminate those things, no scolding and hence no growling."*

I then explained how pleased I was to hear Sharon say that Blackie needn't necessarily sit rather than jump up, since very few people want a dog who has to be commanded to behave acceptably. A quicker and more permanent correction allows the dog to make its own adjustment rather than jump. He thereby 'internalizes' the adjustment, rather than obeys an external command to behave differently.

This led to more questions of Ralph and Jack about objectives and resulted in an excellent, realistic picture of a dog who would be able, reasonably, to satisfy his owners' needs.

Even with the behavioral objectives set, there was no mention of a schedule for meeting them, i.e. He should stop chewing clothing by week 4 jumping by week 2, etc.

Problems usually clear up based more on changing circumstances than on time.

The Ritual Exercise "Track:"

Once the value of ritual in a pet's life (especially dogs) is understood in terms of the security it endows and the opportunity for the owner to take a daily leadership role, most clients are anxious to begin teaching. Every counselor will have a favorite sequence in which to teach commands. For the record, although all my clients did not teach all of these, here is the sequence I found useful.

Note: With a couple of exceptions and variations, this ritual sequence is based on Dare Miller's exercise sequence, which appears in the DogMaster manual, *The Secret of Canine Communication.*

1. Tippy, Come. This started out the "training" section of the sessions each week, using distractions of increasing

intensity and greater distances between client and dog each week.

2. Tippy, Sit. This usually happens in the first *training* session in the second meeting. Once the dog comes 3 times in a row on the first command, the Sit is taught. The release of OK is given after 3-5 seconds, then doubled, re-doubled, etc..., until a 2 minute sit is achieved. Once again, distractions are increased weekly, as with Come.

3. Stay. (No name.) The owner steps forward about 3 feet while turning to face the dog. Standing motionless for about 5 seconds at first, then steps toward and around the dog counter-clockwise to return to the starting position at the dogs right. Then FREE releases.

4. Tippy, Heel. Generally only used with extremely dominant or submissive dogs. Its value lies in teaching small circle-heels, 3-5 feet in diameter. Bossy dogs usually object to left circles, where the owner is on the dominant, outside. Submissive dogs love the left circles, but lag on right circles, which are generally enjoyed by dominants. Whichever needs more improvement is practiced more, at increasing speeds, until both directions are accepted by the dog.

5. Tippy, Down. follows the commands to Sit/Stay. This is usually taught on a mat, which is the dog's 'place' for the "GO" or "Place" part of the ritual exercise. Durations and distractions are increased gradually. OK is the release.

6. Tippy, Place. This is taught starting with the Down at the mat, then OK releasing to a point no more than four dog-lengths from the mat. The dog is praised, then teacher stands and takes a sudden step toward the mat as the "Tippy, Place" is spoken and pointed finger freezes at the mat. Dog usually goes to mat. If not, teacher steps back and repeats command and movements to mat. Dog

is praised at the mat, released with OK. Distance is doubled.

Entire Ritual Exercise:

Each time a new command is introduced, it is tacked-on following the last command of the sequence so far learned. The entire ritual sequence is most beneficial when it is completed within 2 minutes with each family member old enough to perform it.

Training Side-Notes:

- Clients are always rehearsed in teaching each command without the dog present. Lots of praise for both effort and performance is given each student. This avoids exposing the dog to the usual "Klutz Syndrome" displayed by most clients performing for an audience for the first time.

- The clients choose a nick-name for their dog. This is used when talking about, but not to, the dog.

- During the teaching, all commands are initially whispered. Voice is added as distractions require it. This helps to insure response.

- The command "Tippy, Come" is never used except to start the dog's name followed by praise is used.

- The "Tippy, Come" is initially taught by having the client quickly move to a position behind the dog, with the client' left side kept toward the dog for left-side orientation for the Sit and Heel positions.

- Although we use the word "Come" in this text, I recommend using a code word (I like "Koy") because "come" tends to get worn out in casual circumstances around the house.

- The ritual is performed both without and with a leash. The initial teaching is usually done without the leash.

Summarizing the Ritual's Value:

This daily ritual gives the client's program a sequence of attainable goals in addition to solving behavior problems. The exercise can be performed in the home on a daily basis within two minutes, it achieves an invaluable environmental essence of leadership for clients.

The Sixth and "final" Session:

I find it useful to have a sort of ritual on the final meeting. This consists of a review of the program from notes, pointing out goals, progress, any backsliding, etc.

This is followed by all clients putting the dog through their ritual exercises. Then a group photo is taken (a copy to be sent later) with a framed 'Behavior Certificate.'

Our programs are open-ended. That is, if the clients feel they need another meeting for more guidance, it is available at no further fee. Very seldom is this needed, because I learned years ago to recognize and deal with one of counseling's most dangerous pitfalls; dependency.

The Dependency factor:

If clients start telephoning between meetings with questions or reports of behavior which they claim not to understand (but which they should) they may be developing a dependency on the counselor. They need the counselor' support, but not in the way they imagine. The phone call is one symptom of dependency, but more apparent are general principles clients will reveal.

- They want to be 'told' why certain things are happening or what to do in this, that, or the other situation, even though the corrective action called for is the same. When this happens, they need to be 'asked' why things are occurring and what they should do in the situations.

In other words, clients with dependency symptoms should be guided to analyze the problem and decide on corrective steps themselves. A brief example may help illustrate it.

The client was in her third meeting and tended to ask about specific situations regarding problems, one of which was jumping up on people, even though the principle for the correction was the same for each one. She telephoned almost every evening with a new scenario.

"My piano teacher is coming over tomorrow afternoon, and she may bring her 8 year-old daughter with her. Do you think I should put 'Brandy' away?"

"Why would you put her away?"

"Well, the child was a little frightened last month when Brandy ran up to say 'hello.'"

"Yes?"

"Well, I don't want to traumatize the little girl."

"What are the alternatives to putting the dog away?"

"That's what I wanted to talk to you about. I'm not sure I can trust Brandy yet."

"Well, last week you handled things beautifully with your sister's kiddies. How did you do that?"

"Yes, but they know Brandy real well."

"True. But let's run through what you did that worked."

(The client then related how she greeted the nieces and corrected Brandy successfully.)

"Excellent. "You controlled things perfectly. No jumping. No screaming by the children. No panic. And an outstanding job. How's that fit tomorrow?"

"If I can do it, it should be OK."

"Why do you say 'If.'"

"Oh, I'm just nervous, I guess."

"That's perfectly normal. In fact, if you weren't little 'up' for the situation, you'd probably not do so well. Actually, you've analyzed things nicely and come up with the solution. Run through what you're going to do."

(She laid out her actions quite correctly.)

"I'm happy with what you've done and said. And you're the boss. Just follow your own example and I'll see you Saturday."

"All right. I'll get it done. I guess it won't be the end of the world if the lesson has to wait a few minutes."

"I've got a feeling your piano teacher wouldn't bring her daughter along if she really objected to Brandy. In fact, after the previous hassle, she'll probably be tickled to see you handle things, even if it takes a couple of minutes."

"Yeah. She's got an unruly dog herself. She ought to understand."

"So, how do you feel about it now?"

"OK. I'll get it done."

"Great. Because the way you... "

(Client interrupted)... "feel about things affects the way Brandy behaves. I know! (laughs) See you Saturday."

This client improved steadily. She required two telephone follow-ups after her program, but these were more for progress reports than for difficulties.

Most dependencies occur because the client is not applying the principles of their correction programs diligently, with conviction, which is often due to a lack of understanding of the principles. In these cases it is helpful to ask them to review which principles apply to the troublesome situations.

"So you and Fran had the argument. She left for work first, then you took off. And the album cover was ripped up when you got home at 5:30. Why?"

"I haven't played that record in months. Are you telling me we can't even argue any more?"

"What do you think?"

"I think I'm goddam pissed off at 'Harvey,' and I'll be damned if I'm gonna shape my life to pamper his ego."

"That sounds pretty normal to me. But what could you have done differently that might have made everyone feel different before everybody stormed off to work?"

"You mean the 'quiet time'?"

"That's right."

"I probably should've, because I almost ran a stop-light on the way to work, I was so distracted."

"Some quiet might have lowered everybody's blood pressure."

"I guess we better talk about it when she gets home. We'll let you know tomorrow at the meeting."

These clients soon were trouble-shooting their own 'backslides' and making adjustments successfully without developing further dependency.

Summary:

We have covered the basic elements of the six-meeting counseling program, from the underlying concepts of the client-centered approach to the training 'track.' Combined with other recommended texts and their examples, I hope these allow you to develop a mental picture of the framework and the dynamics of successful programs.

8

COUNSELING FAMILIES WITH CHILDREN

The family with children and a problem-dog usually has a few problems in their inter-personal human relationships, too. Counseling about a pet behavior problem does not license us to pry into the exact nature of child-parent and sibling conflicts, but it would be unprofessional to ignore their impact on the animal, or not to offer the family guidance about their effects.

Using RMM's cartooning insight in "Better Behavior in Dogs," I tried to expose most of the important 'types' of home situations which most often create frustration, anxiety and problems. The way a counselor handles these family conflicts when face-to-face with Mom, Dad and the kids is more important than attempting to moderate family discussions about them. We need only to put before the family a general framework of how emotional discord can mess up a pet's perception of its role in the group. But before these appropriate cause-and-effect factors can be related, we need to find out how the children and parents feel about the pet and how they behave around it.

Children Should Attend Sessions

We need everyone there who can understand and/or put into action any needed changes in their relationships with the pet. This might even be an infant whose parents need guidance in teaching the child how to approach and pet dog or cat. Even though the baby does not 'understand' that sticking its finger into the dog's eye may cause a bite, the parents can be coached in teaching the child ways to pet which can at least minimize chances for problems. This is also a prime opportunity to observe parental attitudes regarding child- and/or pet-scolding when the two interact. If guidance is needed, there is no better time, especially if there is disagreement between parents on the subject.

Most children between four years and puberty identify extremely closely with their pets. When the animal is physically punished for some misbehavior the children often cry or even become hysterical. In addition, children often emulate parental examples and punish the pet when the folks aren't around, only to get bitten or scratched as a result. This aspect of family dynamics reinforces the concept that non-punishment corrections not only best fit pet animal species, but also promotes a more harmonious human family life.

Fact-finding meetings with kids

When everyone is seated, following the initial greetings and preliminary interaction with the dog, I have found it helpful to get everyone involved as quickly as possible. This keeps the children occupied and helps develop their interest in the counseling session. Assuming that the fact sheet is fairly complete, it is usually best to start with the most outgoing child somewhat as follows.

"Janet, what do you think about 'Ginger'?"

This generally gets things rolling. However, not all children respond immediately. Many kids are inhibited by the presence of their parents and/or siblings.

Reluctant Children

This is one time, especially with less-talkative children, when a little leading or prompting can be useful. If the child seems to be blocking responses to open-ended, non-directive questions, a statement such as;

"Golly, I'll bet she does something that makes you happy." Or,

"How does Ginger make you happy?"

Conversely, if you are after areas of more specific feelings regarding misbehavior...

"What does Ginger do that you'd rather she didn't?"

Don't Assume the Parents' Role

The counselor's role in meetings is that of a family friend. As such, it is important to avoid "sounding like the folks." Many times when a child is reluctant to answer a question, don't press him of her. Further, if one of the parents wants to urge the child to answer, take a neutral role. Avoid interfering or showing any facial or body language of approval, disapproval or urgency. If the parent wants to insist on an answer, so be it. You might also be witnessing one of the attitudes (insensitivity to a child's feelings of embarrassment, etc.) that could bear on the problem at home as well.

When a child blocks completely, and when the opportunity arises, it is best to tell everyone that you can understand the situation and that you'd like to go on to some other questions. When another family child does answer your questions, the reluctant child often chips in with his or her opinions. Otherwise, you can await another time when the child has been playing or doing an exercise with the dog to ask questions. Kids are usually more talkative after some relaxing physical activity.

Handling Tattle-Tales

Fortunately, few children will be slow to answer questions. In fact, once they start talking it is usually a challenge to get them to stop! Often they will talk about what a brother or sister did (which they think was wrong) before they will let you know the things they themselves did to the dog, either alone or with one of their siblings. At these times it is vital not to appear judgmental. Just look and sound 'interested.' Then, try to redirect things to the child him- or herself so as to take the pressure off the sibling who is being 'ratted-on'.

This type of situation usually comes up in cases involving hyper-sexual and/or aggressive dogs. It is not uncommon to find that some children are embarrassed by a puberty-aged puppy who mounts them or their friends. Often, instead of talking about how they personally react to it, they will 'tell-on' a sibling who tolerates, or even encourages the puppy.

In aggressive cases this sometimes uncovers a child who deliberately 'sics' the dog on other children or teases the dog to the point of exasperated viciousness. The best way to re-direct things back to the 'tattler' is to indicate interest, then resume asking the child doing the talking details about their own behavior. For example:

> *"That often happens, Debbie, and it'll help us later when we talk to Steve. What do you do when "Cranky" tries to mount you?" (or, "growls at friends, etc...")*

This response is non-judgmental, reinforces the child for responding, then gets back to the subject in question without making Steve feel awkward.

However, there will be times when Steve will retaliate with his own testimony about Debbie's behavior. When this happens, it is best to let the talk run its course, releasing control to the parents in case things start to get out of hand. In this event, when the dust settles, you can comment that such events are not rare in your work, and that it is a valuable step in getting at the causes for "Buster's" problems.

Children Jealous of the Dog

Most children regard their pets as siblings, on the one hand, but as outsider-family members on the other, a little like step-brothers or step-sisters, especially if the pet arrived after the children. It is not unusual for child to behave quite differently when alone with a pet than when in the company of other family members. Siblings may argue about and/or vie for Tippy's attention and affection when together, yet ignore her alone. Or, vice versa. Either way, it behooves us to look for signs of contention between children during interviews.

In the event these elements do exist, it is not always necessary to get the kids to go into detail about them, although they should be allowed to if they want. What the counselor needs to do is stress the pet's need for consistency. One way of getting into this area follows.

"How does 'Tippy' act if you kids argue around her?"

Once again, the usually forbidden leading question, However, with kids it is generally effective if it is stated with genuine warmth and without any hint of judgment on the counselor's part. When the answer has been explored, it will reveal that the pet is confused and anxious. This, then, can be related so that the children empathize with the animal.

"I guess 'Tippy' feels about the same as we would if a couple of friends got into a really serious argument... embarrassed and confused. That's why all of our pets need to get the same love and treatment from everybody they live with. What do you think?"

If all this gets is a nod from the children, it is best left to incubate, as an idea must if it is to be effective. If the children want to discuss things, it is best to let them do so. Once again however, if sibling sparks begin to fly, I have found it most effective to let the parents practice their 'parenting' and remain neutral.

Children Are Usually an Asset to Programs

All the foregoing may seem to indicate that children are genuine problems during programs. Actually, their actions, words and their feelings toward their pets are usually so innocent and honest that they generally speed up the process of rehabilitation.

I have had a few, mostly 'only' children, who have seemed to want things to fail. One case is documented in "Behavior Problems in Dogs" and serves as a classic example of this type of situation. Generally, kids identify so closely with their animals that they adjust more quickly than their parents to new ways of perceiving their relationships and, hence, acquiring new attitudes about them.

Should Children Train the Dog?

I have found it helpful at least to get children involved in the "learn-to-earn-praise-and-petting" portion of the programs. This includes kids under the age of five. If the counselor teaches and coaches the children with plenty of praise, getting them to do the same for the dogs, the dogs seem to enjoy it as well.

There is a further benefit to the parents: They see the counselor using successful motivational methods based on non-authoritarian principles, yet effectively gaining the child's enthusiastic participation, and the dog's equally enthusiastic response.

Once again, the counselor is teaching-by-example while the student (parent) has the opportunity to "catch" the counselor's attitude. At the end of meetings I have had many parents say, "Why don't you come home and work with my kids for a few weeks?" To which always respond, "No. I couldn't do it there. I'm not the authority figure there that I am here. Besides, when you apply the same principles, you'll be a far better teacher, anyway." I have seen entire programs turn around and head for success after that one phrase.

Addressing Parents

When parents are with their off-spring they are vulnerable to, and sensitive about, being given advice. It is unwise, for instance, to ask a question or make a statement that might create the impression you disapprove of something they have said or done. This is where being non-judgmental confronts its strongest test.

For example, if Dad describes punishing the dog in a way that is blatantly abusive, it is advisable to nod and move on to another area of discussion. Later in the meeting, if the children can be guided to some activity, such as playtime with the dog, outdoors or in a different room, you can return to the subject and discuss with him what effect he thinks the heavy punishment might have had on the children. At this point, Mom will usually join in discussion, and agreement can be reached about using non-physical alternatives. When this opportunity is not available you will have to ask Dad to phone for a chat during the week.

Summary

Children are usually an essential part of a successful family behavior program. Since they are usually involved in the cause for problems, their participation can accelerate progress in fact-finding, developing remedial steps and carrying out the program at home.

The counselor should be seen as a valued family friend, one who never assumes parental authority, but yields to the parents if the kids begin bickering or are uncooperative during meetings.

Children should also be part of training sessions, since they will be providing a vital consistency in the dog's life at home.

9

SINGLE SESSIONS

I have stressed the word "Program" up to now in the hope that it becomes entrenched as a basic tenet of effective counseling. However, single-shot meetings, which might better be called "Evaluations," do have a place in a behavioral practice, but I never recommend them as an alternative to programs, and rarely mention them, unless the client asks or the situation is unique.

When the Client Asks:

Some clients either cannot afford a program, or do not want to spend the money. In either case, it should be pointed out that a single session allows time only for a preliminary evaluation of their problem and recommended remedies can only be tentative because as the normal six-week correction program progresses the dog and owner's behavior 'evolves' under the guidance of weekly counseling.

Also, the fee for a single session is 1 and 1/2 times the per-meeting fee for a full program. This does not mean that single-shot sessions cannot succeed. Many have done well. However, it is rarely as satisfactory to both client and counselor as a full program.

When these facts are explained, most clients appreciate your candor and will enroll in a program, take a single session, do nothing... or go to someone else who will give them what they want, rather than what they need.

When the Situation is Unique:

Sometimes special circumstances will dictate that you see someone with a dog only once. following are those that have come up in my experience.

- To accommodate another professional who needs a second opinion or an evaluation of a dog. This includes seeing client, breeder, veterinarian, etc..., with a dog who is suspected of being hyper-kinetic, hyper-reactive; has some other minimal brain dysfunction, such as hyperesthesia (shows pain when touched), photo-sensitivity (light/shadow), psychomotor seizure activity (to sounds, shapes, situations etc...), spontaneous aggressiveness.

- Clients with travel problems, who can make only one trip.

- Impaired clients with special problems, such as wheel chair orientation training or blind clients with cat-chasing guide-dogs (for evaluation); etc...

- Demonstrating and teaching orientation-to-owner techniques for clients with deaf or blind dogs.

- Demonstrating puppy selection tests for breeders and clients.

When single sessions are held for referring professionals, I always offer a professional courtesy (20%. discount).

"Brush-up" Single Sessions:

Former clients may call and ask for refreshers on their daily training ritual exercise with a new dog, or simply to discuss some aspect of their dog's behavior. If your programs are not open-ended, this warrants a single session and fee as well.

These kinds of single sessions can usually be held in 60-75 minutes. However, special circumstances may dictate up to three hours, in which case the fees are adjusted accordingly.

10

EUTHANASIA
THE ULTIMATE SOLUTION?

I am often asked if some problems aren't so severe that I recommend euthanasia. I never flatly recommend it, even in cases
where it seems inevitable.

Why Not Mention It?

First, especially in serious problem cases, it has usually been
mentioned by the client during the fact-finding phase.

Secondly, in client-centered counseling, it is not our role to
suggest putting an end to life because of a behavior problem. To
the contrary—it the counselor's duty is to create appreciation by
the client for the pet's uncanny ability to sense that something is
gravely 'wrong' in their relationship, then to motivate clients to a
total commitment to solve the problem. Without this, things
usually get worse.

In the third place, when the counselor introduces euthanasia,
most clients will gain the impression that it deserves serious
consideration, since it came from someone whom they consider
to be an authority.

Except for this chapter's title, euthanasia is not referred to as a *solution*. Putting an animal to death never solves a behavior problem. It terminates a life. While the pet is eradicated, emotional problems are created for the client; feelings of guilt, anger and grief, which are shared by client-centered counselors and the veterinarians or other professionals who must perform the dark deed.

Because of this client-empathy, and in order to cope with these emotions and still function effectively, the counselor needs a realistic attitude about euthanasia.

Euthanasia by Definition:

Euthanasia translates from the Greek as "Good death." It is defined as: "Dying easily, quietly, painlessly."

Euthanasia in Perspective:

First, it helps if we face one fact, eyeball-to-eyeball:

Tippy is killed, no matter how it is sugar-coated with terms like "Putting Tippy to sleep,"

Further, killing an animal because of a behavior problem is not 'kind.' At best, it may be the 'least unkind' thing we can do.

On the surface, this attitude may seem unsympathetic toward pet owners who are faced with one of the grimmest decisions they will ever make. It is neither professional nor necessary to mention these truths to clients. However, many clients have told me that this icy reality is what it all boils down to for them, especially at night, during the sleepless hours when the pet is dead. This is the ultimate, stark, emotional truth. And owners tell me it must be faced before they can accept things as they are and get on with living; the sooner they discard the fairy-tale phrases, the quicker they get down to genuine grieving and allow time and events to ease the pain that will always be felt.

Emotions Vs Words:

Emotions are not spoken words... they are "internal." Words may arouse feelings, but they cannot deceive our 'emotional selves.' Therefore, I never recommend shocking clients with words like "killing," or "death" when the subject of euthanasia is raised. Clients don't need counselors who appear to condone or condemn euthanasia. Rather, they need someone who appears to understand the depth of their dilemma without descriptions of it. I have found that counselors with a realistic view of euthanasia are better able to help their clients face this inner reality. Perhaps this comes across as an 'attitude,' reflected from counselor to client. This may lend some truth to the old adage about an attitude being "caught, not taught." The question is: If it is not helpful to mention it, how can we best expose the client to it?

When Euthanasia Comes Up:

The client who mentions "getting rid" of the dog is usually thinking about euthanasia, finding another home for it, or both. The earlier this is explored during fact-finding, the better. This can be done by asking what they have considered thus far. When euthanasia is mentioned, it can be dealt with in ways aimed at gaining a total commitment to reaching a behavioral solution.

When the client with a mild problem mentions euthanasia, I find it useful to say something to this effect;

> *"I know we can all get so mad that we feel like having him euthanized, but most people agree it's a pretty severe punishment for chewing (or whatever the problem is, even biting) before we've even tried to solve the problem."*

This kind of response introduces the reality and finality of euthanasia and puts it into perspective in relation to the problem. Most clients will agree that something must be done to solve the problem. In the event they don't agree, there are often other viable solutions that can save a life.

Alternatives

Especially in problems that only happen within the client's environment, placing the dog in another home deserves priority over euthanasia. Contrary to popular opinion, behavior problems are not always part of a dogs portable 'baggage.' Further hope lies in contacting pure-breed rescue groups, advertisements on veterinary bulletin boards, calling friends who have expressed affection for the dog. Also, some kennels offer "lifer" boarding services for some problem dogs. All of these should be considered.

Dead-End Situations:

So, what about persistent, vicious biting, fighting, hysterical destructiveness, self-mutilation problems; when all remedies have failed and the client says euthanasia seems to be the only way out?

After examinations and diagnoses for everything from nutritional allergies to hyper-kinesis to hormonal imbalances to brain tumors, etc., along with behavioral therapy, I recommend the following:

Schedule a meeting without the pet present and summarize everything that has been done; then simply say that we have exhausted all our resources. At this point, the most considerate and effective action I have found is silence.

Silence is a 'Sound' policy:

Silence is invaluable. It gives clients time to think about what has been summarized. I have had many clients say they have failed to follow certain aspects of their programs consistently, or sincerely, and that they want to carry on with the program. Not surprisingly, most of these cases have had happy endings.

Silence also allows time for the client to consider the value of the counselor's services. If blame is to be assigned, the client can 'unload' on the counselor. If it happens, and it will, silence is still effective until the client asks questions.

Questions should be answered honestly, non-defensively, and with unspoken empathy for the client's normal tendency to 'displace' self-directed anger toward the counselor.

Here are some statements that clients with biting dogs often make, along with some responses a counselor can make.

"Well, it sure took a lot of time and money to learn that 'Tippy' was a hopeless case."

> *"Jim, I appreciate that, and I wish there were more we could do. If you think there are other steps we can try, or things we should try again, let's consider them."*
> *(Silence)*

This conveys consideration for the client's feelings and leads the client to re-think things and further express himself. He may make suggestions, and they should be given careful consideration. I have had life-saving ideas from clients in some cases. However, the usual clients response concerns euthanasia.

> *"I suppose the only thing left is to have 'Tippy' put to sleep."*

> *"If you feel you've done everything feasible to help 'Tippy,' and ending his life to avoid a disaster is the only remaining alternative, as upsetting as it will be, I can appreciate your consideration of it. If there were another way, I'd suggest we try it."* *(Silence)*

There are numerous variations to these client comments and counselor reactions to the "hopeless" case summary. But these are typical of them. However, there are often alternatives.

Making the Decision:

Clients should never be made to feel rushed when considering euthanasia. One of the most futile and aggravating errors often made by counselors is to try to assure clients that they are doing the "right" thing, or that it is the "kindest" action they can take, or to say "I know how you must be feeling."

Any client who has considered having pet killed knows the following:

- Nothing is "right" anywhere in life at that point.

- Everything is wrong about everything. Nor do they feel they are being kind. They often feel heartless, even cruel.

- Most of all... only the client "knows" how they feel.

Even if you have euthanized your own pet due to a behavior problem it is best not mentioned at this stage... unless the client asks about it.

If the client wants to leave and decide later, this should be reinforced approvingly, with assurance that you want them to call and that you are anxious to help them in any way possible.

When the decision is made during the counseling session, the atmosphere will be charged with emotion. The only advice I have at this stage is to be yourself.

If you have a healthy relationship with your clients, if you have grasped the concept of client-centered counseling, this will be a thoroughly miserable experience for all of you. It would do no good to relate my own feelings in these situations. No words exist for them. Your feelings will be unique to you, they will guide your behavior as you counsel your clients. This is as it should be.

11

THE BUSINESS Of PROFESSIONAL COUNSELING

Most pet behavior counselors aren't generally perceived by their clients as "mercenary" about the financial aspects of their practices. However, we all need to handle our fees and financial affairs so we have clothes, housing, food and transportation if we are going to function effectively in the field. Also, most highly 'people-oriented' people (as a counselor must be) are not usually enamored with record-keeping, so it is fortunate that in this work we can keep paper records to a minimum, make an excellent living and still keep the canis lupus from the IRS at bay.

Let's go through the necessary physical supplies first, and then look at the vital aspects of community and professional contact work that will establish and keep your name and services fresh.

Financial Records:

Spend an hour at a stationery store to find the type of record-keeping aids that appeal to you. These should cover:

- If you are computer wise, the Quicken Home Business bookkeeping program is a dandy, especially if you set it up in concert with the Turbo-Tax IRS program. If not...

- A diary-type bookkeeping book which has an "income" and an "expenses" capacity. Keep this up weekly, if you can, monthly at least.

- A seven day planner/appointment book. Keep daily appointments, pencil in income when it is received, from whom. You can transfer this to you books when needed.

- An auto mileage/expenses log book. Keep this in your car and keep gas and repair receipts in it, as well. Transfer the information as needed to your bookkeeping records.

- 12 large manila envelopes . When expense receipts have been recorded monthly, mark the month on an envelope and put them in there.

If you do your own IRS tax reports, this is really all you need. However, if you use a tax accountant, check with them and use their system

If you have a home office, or if your practice is conducted at home, phone (don't go in) the IRS and explain your situation. Measure both the square footage and the time that is devoted to business and personal use. Do the same for all your utilities, especially the telephone. Ask the IRS for guidelines. If they are not forthcoming, go back to the stationery store and buy the latest IRS tax guide for the self-employed and let that be your guide.

Professional Records:

- An Alphabetized 5 x 8" card file. Go through the Yellow Pages and make a card out for every veterinary clinic, kennel, pound, humane society, pet shop, groomer, trainer and anyone else connected with your type of animal who may deal with your type of clientele.

This is your "referral file." Record each client referred and the date, a cryptic note about the problem and outcome. This will also be used as your guide to contacting these referral people, so leave space for dates of contacts, and note whether it's 'Personal' or by 'Phone.'

- An 81/2 x 11" Alphabetized file Box. This will hold your client record sheets when completed.

Professional Supplies:

- Business Cards. Keep these simple! If you have some kind appropriate degree, use the letters. However, avoid such things as slogans. I use the following card information:

DOG BEHAVIOR SERVICES Sun Valley Ranch

Wm. E. Campbell

By Appointment (541) 476-5775

P.O. Box 1658 Grants Pass, OR 97526

We use a P.0. Box to keep folks from showing up on the doorstep, which we learned the hard way; meaning we've had litters of pups and adult dogs dumped over our driveway gates!

Stationery

Keep it just as simple as the cards. I do have a logo on mine, as you have noted. But no slogans.

Agreement forms.

If you keep dogs on your premises, or if your area is infected by law-suits check with an attorney and follow the advice.

Advertising:

- Yellow Pages. If you want to 'stand out' there, follow the rule: Keep it simple. It is really just a convenience for your referral people, so they can say, "they're in the Yellow Pages." Let the others take the expensive box ads and bold type. Just your name and phone number with no address will do the job.

- Brochures. I used them in the early days in Los Angeles, but found that they did not make a bit of difference in the quality of referrals from veterinarians, pet shops, etc. In fact, they give the prospective client a chance to make a decision about your services independently from any personal discussion of their problem. Therefore, I'd suggest saving the money. Just leave a supply of cards with your referral points.

- Newspapers, etc... I'd save money here, too.

- Public relations. If you can send out behavior tips to newspapers and local magazines, radio and TV stations, do it. Give interviews when requested, but make sure that you give the reporters the same orientation to your services that you give your clients. Most of them will come to you with their stories already written, at least mentally, so your orientation will put them on track and may avoid the old pet-on-the-couch "dog psychiatrist syndrome." Also, keep your tape recorder going in the interviews!

- You may also want to contact local schools and arrange to speak to students about pet care and problems. Don't forget service clubs and the elderly.

- Of course, let your local veterinary association know of your activities and willingness to speak at their meetings.

- The same holds true for humane groups, trainer's associations, boy and girl scouts, etc... If you have 35mm slides of dogs, etc..., which give an idea of your work, use those. Videos are great. If you have them, use them.

Professional Relations:

These are the very foundation of your practice. Most crucial are the relationships you establish with the veterinarians in your area, so I'll outline the method found most successful and leave it to you to adapt it to your own 'style' of presenting your services. The same method will apply to all other referral professionals.

- The Phone Call. Start with the practices nearest to you and work your way out. Dial the number and ask:

"This is (your name). Is Dr. Smith in?"

You'll usually be asked what it's about.

"I'd like to arrange a time when I might spend a few minutes to explain our pet behavior services to him/her and see the clinic (hospital) so I can describe it to my clients who are new to the area and looking for veterinary care."

If you can't get through, ask for a more convenient time to phone. (This will usually be just after noon or before 3:00 pm, pre- or post-surgery times.)

If you get the "we're not interested" answer from the receptionist, make a note on the card and drop by to introduce yourself to that receptionist at a later date. Then go in and re-introduce yourself to them, explaining your services. This personal meeting often breaks the resistance and leads to a chance to speak to the doctor.

If you do get through to the veterinarian, repeat the purpose of your call and set up a time. If you have the budget, invite the doctor to lunch or a cup of coffee, if she/he has the time.

In some situations you'll get clients not referred by a veterinarian you want to get to know. In these cases, when you telephone, mention the client's name and give a brief description of their program. Then say you appreciate a chance to meet the doctor and staff to explain your services.

Visiting the Practice:

At the practice, make sure you see the entire plant, if humanly possible. Ask questions if the doctor says things you don't understand. After all, you're going to ask her/him to learn about your services, so let her/him explain the facilities and services! Avoid any emotionalism about patients. Be professional and adopt a learning attitude. Avoid commenting about euthanasia, the "green needle" or the "body freezer" and disposition of carcasses unless asked for your ideas. If so, give your honest opinions.

- Wait for the doctor to show interest in your activities. Then, explain your services, accentuating the causative approach you use. Don't go into your own background until asked about it. *And you will be asked!*

- Then, give the explanation you use with your clients. Be sure to mention that you send "progress reports" and acknowledge referrals either in writing or by phone. In other words, tell the doctor that you give feedback on referrals.

- Don't stretch the meeting. The doctor is busy and so are you, even if you only have another referral point to call on.

- Thank the doctor for the time, ask if you can leave some cards (brochures) with him or her or at the desk, and bid your leave.

- Be sure to introduce yourself to receptionists, technicians and all people in the practice, if the opportunity comes up. Don't rush around glad-handing people. Just say "Hi," and give your name, what you do, and say it's good to meet them. If they have questions, be just as complete with them as with the doctor.

In the early days of practice you will spend more time making contacts holding client consultations. However, don't fret. If you follow this method you'll soon be so busy that you will be hard-pressed to make these personal calls as often as you would like!

Follow this program with all your referral points and you will be forging the basis of meaningful professional associations with the community.

A "Worst-Case" Veterinary Visit Example:

It may help to describe briefly my very first veterinary contact. It was with the owner/veterinarian of a most successful West L.A. practice. When I introduced myself and said I was the new consultant at the Canine Behavior Center, he said...

"Not another one!"

(Several consultants had preceded me in a matter of months.)

He told me about his experience in obedience training his dogs (while he was cleaning a dog's teeth, by the way) and then asked about my background. I related it to him and he said he'd give me a "try" and judge by the results.

I didn't get a tour of the practice or introductions to staff members and I went out feeling pretty low. However, his first referrals were 'doozies.' One was a 'German Shepherd-Doberman' bitch who bit the boyfriend and had psycho-motor seizures when the family ignored her. The other was a Collie who had bitten his young owner during obedience class on the forced "Down."

The 'Sheperman' straightened out nicely with the program and the Collie turned up with hip dysplasia, (I noticed hock-rotation when he chased a ball and evidence of pain when he "Downed" by standing from a "Sit" position before he lowered his front end first, then plunked his rear end. (He knew the command... but it was the only way he could get down without pain.)

That veterinarian and his multi-veterinarian practice were pivotal in my practice throughout many years in L.A.

The point is, you can never tell about your effectiveness until you begin working with clients. Then, the quality of your work will speak for you!

Follow-up:

Be sure to phone and acknowledge referrals, at least within a day of the referral. Don't insist on talking to the doctor. Just touch base, so to speak, with the practice. Mail a personal note of thanks to the doctor or other referring professional in the event a personal contact is inconvenient.

When the case is finished, mail a brief summary of it. If it succeeded, explain why. If it "bombed," explain why you think it did so. Never cop-out on the client or the dog. Just explain why it did not succeed. (It is usually that you were not able to "reach" the client in consultation.) After all... this is the truth, at least in client-centered counseling. So face it, and don't worry about it. Your referral professional will understand. He or she has been in the same boat, many times!

Professional Organization Memberships:

The benefit of joining organizations is in keeping informed about the state of the 'art.' While you can gain information, you may also contribute through some associations that have publications which seek membership input. Look up their home pages on the internet and make inquires on line.

- Animal Behavior Society

- American Veterinary Society of Animal Behavior

- Your local veterinary association may offer affiliate memberships to professional non-veterinarians working with veterinary members on behavior. Ask about this.

- Association of Pet Dog Trainers: Holds annual trade shows with speakers.

Publications :

Animal Behavior Consultant Newsletter - $6.00 year
Mercer University
Dept. Psychology
1400 Coleman Ave.
Macon, GA 31207-0001
Keep up on what the behaviorists are talking about.

Whole Dog Journal - $39 annual - 12 issues
PO Box 420235
Palm Coast, FL 32142
Excellent source for holistic health and behavior information.

Pet Behavior Newsletter $30 per calendar year. 4 issues
PO Box 1658
Grants Pass OR 97528
Concentrates on recent advances, or retreats, in the field.

Which brings us to the final publication... yours.

Your Own "Publications:"

Type (or have neatly typed) on your letterhead a "Case of the Month." Keep it to one, single page. No More! Get it copied and send it to veterinarians and other referral professionals in your area. I recommend the following format because it's simple to read and presents only the relevant information.

Behavioral Case of the Month

Problem: Dog: Breed, age, sex, neuter status, size (if not apparent from breed description.

Client situation: (Not by name!) family, housing, etc.

Problem cause: Give your diagnosis.

Remedial program: Describe what you got the clients to do to solve the problem.

Outcome: Give the facts. If outcome pending, say so.

Either mail or drop cases off to your referral points and the local veterinary associations. When you think you have an unusual one, spend a few extra cents and mail copies to publications which may be interested in publishing it. Who knows? You may be offered a regular column!

Your Fees:

I won't offer any advice here, except to mention this: If you pay someone more per hour to fix a broken water pipe than you charge for your professional services, you'd better re-examine your fee schedule.

Finally:

When you follow this program to establish yourself in your community, you'll find, at least for the first few months, that there is a lot more "busy-ness" than "business" in your activities. But just remember, this is a field where you will be working mainly with other people's clients. Your professionalism reflects on them and can enhance or damage their business. Therefore, be prepared to 'pay your dues,' so to speak. Be patient. Let your referral contacts and the professional community know about your successful cases and they will speak for you.

12

COUNSELING SELF-STUDY GUIDE

I first envisaged this guide as an exhaustive citation list of all the literature I have consumed over the last forty-five years; studies that ranged from psychology to physio-nutritional effects on behavior, including hypnosis, neuro-physiology, job study, interviewing, management training, employee motivation, animal training, and sociology. However, experience and advice from some noted educators cautioned me against it. For one thing, I have surely missed some extremely valuable writers and topics, so I would risk limiting the style of study I prize most highly— independent investigation. (In spite of this, I'll mention quite a few favorite authors and texts later.)

The compelling advantage of independent study is in pursuing subjects which keep the student highly motivated. A disadvantage is that there is no friendly, scholarly advisor at your elbow to save you from charging down literature's numerous blind alleys. You are on your own to waste some time. However, many learning theorists maintain that learning anything without making errors merely proves that you knew the answers before you started, or you "lucked out" and got things right. In other words, errors help you learn how to avoid wasting time.

In any event, if you have the time and are motivated to investigate books and journals, here are some principles I have found most helpful. It is not a guide for "what to study." It is a way of deciding what to study *next*.

Which Information Source?

The best source is a university 'bio-medical' library. Next best is a university psychology library. Third is either the main city or county library. However, if you cannot get to any of these, your branch library has a reference clerk who can get practically any book you want, including copies of journals from almost all fields of endeavor. Even better, the internet now affords access to many original papers in the literature. However, unless you are fully familiar with the various types of computer search programs, I can save you lots of time with this advice: Take a crash course in searching for, downloading and printing information.

If you desire to check out books and papers from a university library and are neither a student nor a patron of the school, find someone who is and use their card. It will be worth it. Having adequate time to study at home is better than spending hours in the "wooden chair," burdened by library hours.

Where to Start?

Start with the "Now." That is, begin by reading the latest work on the subject. However, make sure the authors were considerate enough to present references and citations to other authors who have helped them form ideas, base facts, etc. I would not ignore authors who simply write from experience with no references. However, in any field of study, the most useful texts are those which allow you to look into the background of the ideas. I am always amazed at how often my interpretation of an author's source information is at odds with that author's interpretations.

Where Next? Notes

As you read, make notes of the author, title, page numbers, etc., on those things about which you'd like to know more. If the author gives references, note them. Get those texts next and study them. Then, apply the same technique to those writings.

Putting It to Work:

Here's an example from our list. You may want to read some of the referenced authors which will lead to further studies from their own citations.

You might be curious about "Halo, Valid of Invalid," since it is not explained extensively in my books. If you'll get the master directory for 1939's Journal of Applied Psychology, you will be fascinated to learn about how 'halo' actually affects people.

When you get around to Potter's "An Introduction to Therapeutic Counseling" you will see how it fits into actual work with real clients. Then, the next time you are in a session with a client who is trying to get you to agree with some line of reasoning they are using, you'll recognize the 'signs' (nodding at you... awaiting your return nod; or saying "Don't you think?" and awaiting your affirmative nod, response, silence with eye-signs of approval) and you'll know how to handle it more effectively than depending entirely on your intuition.

Actually, the Truax and Carkhuff text cited in this handbook is an excellent source for learning about many useful counseling techniques. Even among those, you'll find helpful citations to earlier works.

Free-wheeling, self-directed study can fill the needs of independent professionals who desire to broaden areas of knowledge or investigate new ones. It also has other advantages if you find an area in which a formal course of university study is desired and a degree is the object. Many schools have programs which give credit for previous experience and study. You might be able to accelerate your study program with the guidance of an educational counselor. Whatever the objective, you should find this approach to studying highly effective.

If you feel the need for actual training in counseling techniques, most universities and community colleges have courses available. After years of training in employee counseling and designing training programs for management personnel, I always recommend programs which include group 'role-playing.' It gives you a chance to experience both the 'counselor' and the 'counseled' perspectives——a most enlightening experience, especially if the group engages in post-session critiques! These sessions in themselves lead to invaluable personal insight and provide unique examples of group dynamics.

A combined behavioral/practice/study program will not only be motivational, but your retention of the knowledge will excel as you apply it afterward with clients.

Notable Authors and Books

The following books contain information that can help clarify thinking about some of the 'fuzzy notions' that are rampant today among both practitioners and academics in the behavioral fields. For instance, all sorts of intellectual debate and confusion exists today regarding operational definitions of "dominance" and "leadership." I have even seen highly educated behaviorists state that they no longer even introduce the concepts to clients, due to the public's confusion about the terms. Yet, going back only to the 1950s and 60s, reading *The Behavior of Domestic Animals,* edited by E.S.E. Hafez, you'll find no confusion about the terms: They were defined elegantly:

- Leader animals *lead* the other animals in the group.

- Dominant animals *drive* the other animals in the group.

In terms applicable to clients and their dogs, I have yet to find an owner who fails to grasp the idea that teaching 'Tippy' to do (or not do) a certain behavior by *making* her do it using physical force or fear, is dominance; while *guiding* her to do it, using movement, stance, a sound, etc., is leadership. Not only do clients grasp the concept, they apply it enthusiastically.

John Paul Scott's writings are also elucidating because he, too, effectively defines and describes dominance and leadership, at the same time creating a clear understanding about aggression between animals of a species, and between humans and animals.

The following list isn't a complete guide, but it provides a valuable starting point for independent study.

Authors/Books

Pfaffenberger, Clarence: The New Knowledge of Dog Behavior, Howell Book House, 1963

Donald R. Griffin: Animal Minds, U. Chi. Press, 1992

Stel'makh, L: Pavlov J Higher Nervous Activity 2:216, 1958.

Melzak, RA and Scott TH: Journal of Comparative Physiology Psychology 50:155-161, 1957.

Fox, MW: Understanding Your Dog. Coward, McCann & Geohegan, New York, 1972.

Pavlov, IP: Conditioned Reflexes. Oxford University Press, London, 1927.

Rech, RH and Moore KE: An Introduction to Psychopharmacology. Raven Press, New York, 1971.

Bowman, RE and Datta, SP: Biochemistry of the Brain and Behavior. Plenum Press, New York, 1970.

Flynn, JP, in Glass DC: Neurophysiology and Emotion. Rockefeller Univ Press, New York, 1967.

Naumenko, EV: Central Regulation of the Pituitary-Adrenal Complex. Consultants Bureau, New York, 1973.

Greenfield, NS and Sternbach RA: Handbook of Psychophysiology. Holt, Rinehart, Winston, New York, 1972.10.

Konorski, J: Integrative Activity of the Brain. Univ Chicago Press, Chicago, 1967.1

Fox, MW: Canine Behavior. Charles C Thomas, Springfield, IL, 1965.

Scott, JP and Fuller, JL: Dog Behavior: The Genetic Basis. Univ Chicago Press, Chicago, 1974.

Rusinov, VS: Electrophysiology of the Central Nervous System. Consultants Bureau, New York, 1973.

Thorndike, EL: Animal Intelligence. Macmillan, New York, 1911.

Skinner, BF: The Behavior of Organisms. Appleton-Century, New York, 1938.

Miller, D: Dog Master Manual. CA, 1987.

Hoerlein, BF: Canine Neurology. Saunders, Philadelphia, 1971.

Lopez, BH: Of Wolves and Men. Charles Scribner's Sons, New York, 1978.

Allen, DL: Wolves of Minong. Houghton Mifflin, Boston, 1979

Beerda, B. Stress and Well-being in Dogs. Utrecht Univeristy, The Netherlands, 1997

Shook, L. The Puppy Report. Lyons and Buford, 1992.

Beck, A. and Katcher, A. Between Pets and People. Purdue University Press, 1996.

Scott, J.P. Aggression. University of Chicago Press, 1975

Delgado JR: Physical Control of the Mind. Harper & Row, New York, 1969.

Rosenblith, WA: Principles of Sensory Communication, A Symposium. M.I.T. Press & John Wiley, New York, 1961.

Sokolov, EN: Perception and the Conditioned Reflex. Pergamon Press, New York, 1963.

Papez, JW: Comparative Neurology. Crowell, New York, 1929.

von Bekesy, G: Sensory Inhibition. Princeton Univ Press, Princeton, NJ, 1966.

Zeigler, HP and Gross CG: Readings in Physiological Psychology. Vol 1, Neurophysiology/Sensory Processes. Harper & Row, New York, 1969.

Pribram, K: Languages of the Brain. Prentice-Hall, Englewood Cliffs, NJ, 1971.

Sutherland, MS and Mackintosh, NJ: Mechanisms of Animal Discrimination and Learning. Academic Press, New York, 1971.

Anderson, AC and Good, LS: The Beagle as an Experimental Dog. Iowa State Univ Press, Ames, 1970.

Clemente, CD and Lindsley DB: Brain Function, v. 5, Aggression and Defense: Neural Mechanisms and Social Patterns. Univ Calif Press, Berkeley, 1967.

Garattini, S and Sigg EB: Biology of Aggression. Interscience Publishers, New York, 1969.

Klosovski, BN: Excitatory and Inhibitory States of the Brain. Israel Program for Scientific Translations, Jerusalem, 1963.

Klosovski, BN: Development of the Nervous System and Its Disturbance by Harmful Factors. Macmillan, New York, 1963.

Zubek, JP: Sensory Deprivation. Appleton-Century-Crofts, New York, 1969.

Truax, C.B. & Carkhuff, R.R.; Toward Effective Counseling and Psychotherapy, Aldine, Pub. Co. Chicago, 1966.

Heiman, M: The relationship between man and dog. Psychoanalytical Quarterly 25:568-585, 1956.

Burke, WF: Children's thoughts, reactions and feelings toward pet dogs. J Genetic Psychology 10:489, 1903.

Bossard, J: The mental hygiene of owning a dog. Mental Hygiene 28:408-413, 1944.

Jung, C: Psychological Types. Kegan Paul, New York, 1938.

Okun, Barbara F: Effective Helping: Interviewing and Counseling Techniques. Brooks-Col, 1996

Brady, John: The Craft of Interviewing. Random House, Inc. 1977

Porter, EH Jr: An Introduction to Therapeutic Counseling. Houghton Mifflin, Boston, 1950.

Slater, E: Patterns of Marriage. Cassell, London, 195

Bingham, W: Halo, valid and invalid. J Applied Psychology, 1939.

Coch, L: Overcoming resistance to change.. J Human Relations, 1:512-53

Tindall, R: The use of silence as a technique in counselling. J Clinical Psychology 3, 1947.

Strodtbeck, F: Husband-wife interaction over revealed differences. J Am Social Review 16:468-473, 1951.

Tagiuri, R et al: Person, Perception and Interpersonal Behavior. Stanford Univ Press, Stanford, CA, 1958.

Plechner, AJ and Zucker M: Pet Allergies. Very Healthy Enterprises, Inglewood, CA, 1986.

Wyrwica W: Mechanisms of Conditioned Behavior. Charles C Thomas, Springfield, IL, 197

Pavlov, IP: Conditioned Reflexes. Oxford Univ Press, London, 1927.

Dumenko, VN: Electrophysiology of the Central Nervous System. Consultant Bureau, New York, 1970.

Ganong and Martini: Neuroendocrinology. Vol 2

Academic Press, New York, 1966.

Naumenko, EV: Central Control of the Pituitary-Adrenal Complex. Consultant Bureau, 1973

Sawyer, CH and Gorski RA: Steroid Hormones and Brain Function. Univ California Press, Berkeley, 197

Valzelli, L: Psychopharmacology. Spectrum Publishers, Flushing, NY, 1973.

Krushinskii, LV: Animal Behavior. Consultant Bureau, 1973.

Scott, JP: Animal Behavior. Univ Chicago Press, 1972.1

Wilson, EO, in: Animal Engineering. Freeman Co, San Francisco, 1974.

Corson, SA et al: Centennial Symposium on Huntington's Chorea. Raven Press, New York,1973.

Hallgren, Spinal Anomolies in Dogs, Animal Behavior Consultant Newsletter, Vol. 9 No. 3, July, 1992.18.

Milani, Myrna M., The Art of Veterinary Practice, U. Penn. Press, 1995

Beaver, Bonnie B., The Veterinarian's Encyclopedia of Animal Behavior, Iowa St. U. Press, 1994.2

Dodman, Nicholas H., BVMS, MRCVS, DVA, Dipl. ACVA and Shuster, Louis, PhD, Pharmacological approaches to managing behavior problems in small animals, Veterinary Medicine, October, 1994.

Feingold, BF: Why Your Child Is Hyperkinetic. Random House, New York, 1974.

Lat, J, in Kare MR: The Chemical Senses and Nutrition. Johns Hopkins Univ Press, Baltimore, 1967.

Fernstrom, JD and Wurtman, RJ: Nutrition, Science, Feb, 1974.

Plechner, AJ and Zucker, M: Pet Allergies. Very Healthy Enterprises, Inglewood, CA, 1986.

Goodman, LS and Gilman, AG: The Pharmacological Basis of Therapeutics. 6th ed. Macmillan, New York, 1980.

Wurtman, RJ: Nutrients that modify brain function. Scientific American, 1982.

Rosenburg, GS and Davis, KL: The use of cholinergic precursors in neuropsychiatric diseases. Am J Clinical Nutrition, Oct, 1982.

Harless, SJ and Turbes, CC: Choline loading: specific dietary supplementation for modifying neurologic and behavioral disorders in dogs and cats. Vet Med/Small Animal Clinician, Aug, 1982.

Kronfeld, DS, Canine and Feline Nutrition, Modern Veterinary Practice. Vols. 57/1,2,3, 1976.

Nutritional Abstract Review. 13:323, 1944. 1

Volhard, W. & Brown, K: The Holistic Guide for a Healthy Dog, Howell Book House, 1995.

These books contain both information and citations that have brought important insights to many professionals in the pet dog behavior fields. They will provide an excellent literary springboard for anyone's self-study.

Enjoy the experience!

EPILOGUE

After re-reading this text countless times, it occurred to me that it lacks specific mention about certain things:

- How do you deal with a client who wants "instant, off-leash control" so they can walk their runaway, unruly dog-fighter, child-biter, car-chaser, etc., with confidence that such misbehavior will not occur, or re-occur?

- What about the client who refuses to allow the house soiling or chewing dog or cat the freedom of the house when they are away from home?

However, these questions are covered in "Behavior Problems in Dogs-3rd ed." and "Better Behavior in Dogs-3rd ed." or by that age-old quote about teaching which appears in "Counseling Programs," chapter 7. Even so, it might help to analyze and discuss in more detail the general subject that is opened in the first question above.

The client who wants instant, off-leash control of a potentially dangerous dog doesn't only want to have his cake and eat it, too. He is violating the laws of most communities and adding fuel to the forces who want to outlaw dog ownership in many cities. His viewpoint is not only dangerous to himself and others, (including his dog), but is awash in irresponsibility.

The "solution" to this type of client's situation lies in counseling that motivates the owner to change his attitude about his responsibilities. In other words, we need to differentiate in our minds between client-wants and client-needs, and apply our skills to bring new insights to this kind of client.

There are those in this field who use and sell devices ranging from choke and prong collars to electrical shock-collars as a means of off-leash training or containing dogs in the yard. However, the reality of the average dog-owner's dilemma of "wants versus needs" begs for a counselor who will help that client recognize that dilemma, deal with it, and then become a responsible dog owner in a society that is becoming alarmingly more anti-dog due to irresponsible pet owners and distorted media coverage regarding dangerous breeds.

I regard people who prey on human weakness as *hucksters* because these devices are not 100% effective, and because they feed on human selfishness. Further, they utilize a mechanistic "ends-justifies-the-means" mentality in man's relationships with one of his oldest mammalian partners, the dog.

I have explained the essence of this viewpoint to many clients during our preliminary discussions of problems, and the vast majority agree; when an owner must rely on painful, artificial control of a pet dog, something is terribly lacking. Very few really want a dog who comes when called simply because they, the owners, represent a means of escaping 250 volts of electric shock to the throat.

For the second question; dealing with clients who don't think they can "trust" the pet in the house alone; that's why our pro-grams span six weeks. Trust takes time, especially when a pet has ruined the owner's belongings or bitten someone. However, coupled with a sincere committment to keep the dog, patience brings progress in stages, and most clients with such pets require plenty of patience and more than a single meeting before their confidence and trust develop fully.

Finally, I think we have covered everything intended in this client-centered counseling guide. If you have finished the studies outlined earlier, if you will focus your attention on the clients and the relationships between them and their pets, if you will apply humane corrective programs, and if you have grasped the essence of client-centered counseling, then you will find your experience as a behavior counselor will richly reward all of your human needs, maybe even some of your "wants."

Kindest regards,

Wm. E. Campbell

Index

G

Golden Rule, 17
Grandin, T. 101
Griffin, D.R., 101
guarantee, 26

H

health, 24

I

interviewing
    controlling Vs leading, 16
    directive, 12
    echo, 36
    halo, 38
    mirror, 37
    non-directive, 14

K

Katcher, A., 101

L

leadership, 58
    and frustration, 58
Lopez, Barry, 101

M

meetings, 45
    equipment, 47
    seating, 46
    space, 46
    training, 46
    who attends, 45
Milani, M.M., 101
mirror, 37

N

needs Vs wants, 17

O

OFF syndrome, 36
operational information, 31

P, Q

perspectives,
    client's, 1
    counselor's 7,
    counselor's on dogs, 8
Pfaffenberger, C., 101
praise, principle of, 57
professional relations, 90-94
programs, counseling, 51
    brush-up sessions, 80
    graduation certificates, 50
    objectives, 62
    ritual exercise track, 64
    single sessions, 79
    six sessions, 61
professional inventory, 20
publications, 94-95

questioning techniques, 30, 36

R

responsibility
    owner's, 25
    shared with counselor, 25

S

Scott, J.P., 101
shock, electric, 104
single sessions, 79-80
    brush-up, 80
    fees, 79
social needs, 9

dogs, 9
study guide, 97-101

T

teaching, essence of, 51-53
telephone 49
telephone, cellular, 49
training, 26, 46

V

veterinary
    examinations, 24
    health, 24
    professional visits, 90

W, X, Y, Z

wants
    human, Vs needs, 11, 104